- Go to **awmi.net/sg423** to download PDFs of the following resources for each lesson in this study guide:
  - Outlines
  - Discipleship Questions
  - Scriptures

- Share as many copies as you'd like.

- These documents are not for resale.

THE
NEW YOU
& THE
HOLY SPIRIT

Study Guide

Andrew Wommack

Unless otherwise indicated, all Scripture quotations are taken from the *King James Version* of the Bible.

The New You & The Holy Spirit Study Guide
ISBN: 978-1-59548-553-3

Copyright © 2012 by Andrew Wommack Ministries Inc.
PO Box 3333
Colorado Springs CO 80934-3333

Published by Andrew Wommack Ministries Inc.

THE NEW YOU

THE HOLY SPIRIT

HOW TO USE YOUR STUDY GUIDE

Whether you are teaching a class, leading a small group, discipling an individual, or studying on your own, this study guide is designed for you! Here's how it works:

Each lesson consists of the **Lesson** text, **Outline**, **Teacher's Guide**, **Discipleship Questions**, **Answer Key**, and **Scriptures**. Some lessons also have additional information.

Outline for Group Study:
I.   If possible, briefly review the previous lesson by going over the **Answer Key/Teacher's Guide** answers for the **Discipleship Questions/Teacher's Guide** questions.

II. Read the current **Lesson** text or **Teacher's Guide** aloud.
   A. Be sure that each student has a copy of the **Outline**.
   B. While the **Lesson** text or **Teacher's Guide** is being read, students should use their **Outlines** to follow along.

III. Once the **Lesson** text or **Teacher's Guide** is read, facilitate discussion and study using the **Discipleship Questions/Teacher's Guide** questions (all questions are the same).
   A. Read one question at a time.
   B. The group should use their **Outlines** to assist with answering the questions.
   C. Have the group read aloud each specifically mentioned scripture before answering the question.
   D. Discuss the answer/point from the **Lesson** text as desired.
   E. As much as possible, keep the discussion centered on the scriptures and the **Lesson** text or **Teacher's Guide** points at hand.
   F. Remember, the goal is understanding (Matt. 13:19).
   G. One individual should not dominate the discussion; instead, try to draw out the quieter ones for the group conversation.
   H. Repeat the process until all of the questions are discussed/answered.

Materials Needed:
Study guide, Bible, and enough copies of the **Outline**, **Discipleship Questions**, and **Scriptures** for each student. (PDFs of the **Outlines**, **Discipleship Questions**, and **Scriptures** can be downloaded via the URL located on the first page of this study guide.)

Outline for Personal Study:
I.   Read the current **Lesson** text or **Teacher's Guide**.
   A. Read additional information, if provided.
   B. Meditate on the given scriptures as desired.

II. Answer the corresponding **Discipleship Questions/Teacher's Guide** questions.

III. Check your work with the **Answer Key/Teacher's Guide** answers.

Materials Needed:
Study guide, Bible, and a writing utensil.

THE
NEW
YOU

INTRODUCTION
—— PART I ——

Choosing to receive Jesus Christ as your Lord and Savior is the most important decision you'll ever make. This book will help you understand the choice you've made and discover what's next.

Welcome to the family!

UNDERSTAND YOUR SALVATION

When God's Word first comes to you, Satan immediately tries to steal it (Matt. 13:19). However, he can only do so if you don't have understanding. That's why you need to comprehend what takes place the moment you accept the Lord. Understanding prevents the devil from talking you out of your salvation benefits.

God's Word promises **"that if thou shalt confess with thy mouth the Lord Jesus, and shalt believe in thine heart that God hath raised him from the dead, thou shalt be saved. For with the heart man believeth unto righteousness; and with the mouth confession is made unto salvation"** (Rom. 10:9-10). **"For whosoever shall call upon the name of the Lord shall be saved"** (Rom. 10:13).

Have you done this? Have you confessed with your mouth the Lord Jesus? Do you believe in your heart that God raised Him from the dead? Are you a **"whosoever"** who has called on the name of the Lord? If your answer is yes, then you've been saved!

You were saved the very moment you sincerely committed your life to Jesus Christ. The truth of His Word instantly came to pass as you believed in your heart and confessed with your mouth. Congratulations—you've been saved!

GOD KEEPS HIS WORD

You're in good hands now!

John 10:28-29 says,

> *I give unto them eternal life; and they shall never perish, neither shall any man pluck them out of my hand. My Father, which gave them me, is greater than all; and no man is able to pluck them out of my Father's hand.*

Since you've committed your life to Him, He'll keep you.

> *For the which cause I also suffer these things: nevertheless I am not ashamed: for I know whom I have believed, and am persuaded that he is able to keep that which I have committed unto him against that day.*
> 2 TIMOTHY 1:12

God will be faithful even when you aren't! **"It is a faithful saying: For if we be dead with him, we shall also live with him: If we suffer, we shall also reign with him: if we deny him, he also will deny us: If we believe not, yet he abideth faithful: he cannot deny himself"** (2 Tim. 2:11-13). When you make mistakes or feel discouraged, just remember—God can't deny Himself, because He always keeps His Word!

KNOWLEDGE UNLOCKS EXPERIENCE

Knowledge from God's Word helps you comprehend what took place in your life at salvation. You began an eternal relationship with the most wonderful Person in the universe. Knowing and following Him will bring you unspeakable joy. Salvation isn't just going to heaven when you die; God wants you to start experiencing your salvation benefits immediately. This requires knowledge from His Word. As you understand and act on that knowledge, you'll experience the benefits of your salvation.

God has given you everything you need for life and godliness through the knowledge of Him.

> *Grace and peace be multiplied unto you through the knowledge of God,
> and of Jesus our Lord, According as his divine power hath given unto us
> all things that pertain unto life and godliness, through the knowledge of
> him that hath called us to glory and virtue: Whereby are given unto us
> exceeding great and precious promises: that by these ye might be partakers
> of the divine nature, having escaped the corruption that is in the world
> through lust.*
>
> 2 PETER 1:2-4

The knowledge of God gives you access to His promises. By believing and acting on them, you'll partake of His divine nature. This means you'll experience all of God's love, joy, peace, health, deliverance, prosperity, etc., that's already in your spirit now by Christ Jesus!

As your thinking changes to line up with your born-again spirit, your life will change too. For instance, perhaps you've spent your entire life hating Mondays. You've always given it over to the devil by believing, speaking, and expecting it to be a bad day. Just because you were born again doesn't mean that all of your negative attitudes and thought patterns have changed yet. Monday will be the same as before until knowledge from God's Word causes you to understand and act differently toward it. As the Word changes the way you believe, speak, and expect things to be, you'll start experiencing your salvation benefits—even on Mondays!

RENEW YOUR MIND!

Your whole outlook will change as you grow in the knowledge of God and His promises. This is called "renewing your mind."

> *I beseech you therefore, brethren, by the mercies of God, that ye present
> your bodies a living sacrifice, holy, acceptable unto God, which is your
> reasonable service. And be not conformed to this world: but be ye
> transformed by the renewing of your mind, that ye may prove what is that
> good, and acceptable, and perfect, will of God.*
>
> ROMANS 12:1-2

The way you think must match your born-again spirit. At salvation, your spirit became an entirely new creation. **"Therefore if any man be in Christ, he is a new creature: old things are passed away; behold, all things are become new"** (2 Cor. 5:17). Your born-again spirit is always in agreement with God. The Word will renew your mind to what's already happened in your spirit.

God wants you to think and act like Him. By submitting yourself to His Word, your life will change like a caterpillar transforming into a beautiful butterfly. Don't allow worldly pressure to squeeze you into its ungodly mold. Renew your mind. Be transformed by the knowledge of God, and your life will increasingly reflect Christ Jesus.

YOUR SPIRIT CHANGED

Some people don't understand the spiritual nature of the radical change that occurred when they committed their lives to Christ. For example, many individuals receive Jesus in jail because they're desperate for a change. Waking up the next morning, they find themselves in the same cell, wearing the same clothes, and eating the same food. They don't feel any different, and their circumstances certainly haven't changed. Discouraged by this lack of immediate outward transformation, they incorrectly conclude that nothing really happened at salvation. Because of this, many never go on to renew their minds and enjoy the benefits of salvation.

Your body and soul (mind, will, and emotions) didn't change at salvation the way your spirit did. If you were fat when you were born again, you were fat afterward. If you were bad at math before you being saved, you'll stay bad at math until you increase in learning. Your mind isn't instantly changed; it's your spirit that's been made new!

Since you can't see or touch your spirit, God's Word is the only way you can know what has happened within. **"It is the spirit that quickeneth; the flesh profiteth nothing: the words that I speak unto you, they are spirit, and they are life"** (John 6:63). Faith is simply trusting what the Word says happened in your spirit more than what you see in the natural.

TRUST THE TRUTH

When I accepted the Lord as an eight-year-old, all I experienced was an inward "knowing." A nagging fear of hell left, but other than that, nothing felt different to me. There were no bells, no whistles, no fireworks. I had to believe God's Word when it said my salvation was true. As I renewed my mind, I increasingly partook of His divine nature and enjoyed living in His promises.

Feelings change, but the truth doesn't! If you genuinely committed your life to the Lord, the truth is He will always honor that commitment. He'll never deny, leave, or forsake you (Matt. 10:32 and Heb. 13:5). Your relationship with God is secure. Whether you felt anything or not, radical change took place in your spirit, and you're now a brand-new person. Trust that God's Word to you is true!

You'll experience your salvation more as you renew your mind. When you think according to the flesh (i.e., what your five senses tell you) and give in to negative external influences, you won't be able to enjoy God's benefits. However, as you trust the truth of God's Word by keeping your mind on the Lord and thinking in line with your born-again spirit, you'll experience God's love, peace, joy, etc. (Gal. 5:22-23). The choice is yours. Begin renewing your mind today!

—— OUTLINE ——

I.   When God's Word first comes to you, Satan immediately tries to steal it (Matt. 13:19).

   A. However, he can only do so if you don't have understanding.

   B. That's why you need to comprehend what takes place the moment you accept the Lord.

   C. Understanding prevents the devil from talking you out of your salvation benefits.

II. God's Word promises **"that if thou shalt confess with thy mouth the Lord Jesus, and shalt believe in thine heart that God hath raised him from the dead, thou shalt be saved. For with the heart man believeth unto righteousness; and with the mouth confession is made unto salvation"** (Rom. 10:9-10).

   A. **"For whosoever shall call upon the name of the Lord shall be saved"** (Rom. 10:13).

   B. Have you done this?

   C. If your answer is yes, then you've been saved!

   D. You were saved the very moment you sincerely committed your life to Jesus Christ.

   E. The truth of His Word instantly came to pass as you believed in your heart and confessed with your mouth.

III. You're in good hands now!

   A. John 10:28-29 says,

   I give unto them eternal life; and they shall never perish, neither shall any man pluck them out of my hand. My Father, which gave them me, is greater than all; and no man is able to pluck them out of my Father's hand.

   B. Since you've committed your life to Him, He'll keep you.

   For the which cause I also suffer these things: nevertheless I am not ashamed: for I know whom I have believed, and am persuaded that he is able to keep that which I have committed unto him against that day.
                                                                    2 TIMOTHY 1:12

   C. God will be faithful even when you aren't!

   It is a faithful saying: For if we be dead with him, we shall also live with him: If we suffer, we shall also reign with him: if we deny him, he also will deny us: If we believe not, yet he abideth faithful: he cannot deny himself.
                                                                    2 TIMOTHY 2:11-13

D. When you make mistakes or feel discouraged, just remember—God can't deny Himself, because He always keeps His Word!

IV. Knowledge from God's Word helps you comprehend what took place in your life at salvation.

A. Knowing and following Him will bring you unspeakable joy.

B. Salvation isn't just going to heaven when you die; God wants you to start experiencing your salvation benefits immediately.

C. This requires knowledge from His Word.

D. As you understand and act on that knowledge, you'll experience the benefits of your salvation.

V. God has given you everything you need for life and godliness through the knowledge of Him.

Grace and peace be multiplied unto you through the knowledge of God, and of Jesus our Lord, According as his divine power hath given unto us all things that pertain unto life and godliness, through the knowledge of him that hath called us to glory and virtue: Whereby are given unto us exceeding great and precious promises: that by these ye might be partakers of the divine nature, having escaped the corruption that is in the world through lust.

2 PETER 1:2-4

A. The knowledge of God gives you access to His promises.

B. By believing and acting on them, you'll partake of His divine nature.

C. This means you'll experience all of God's love, joy, peace, health, deliverance, prosperity, etc., that's already in your spirit now by Christ Jesus!

D. As your thinking changes to line up with your born-again spirit, your life will change too.

E. Just because you were born again doesn't mean that all of your negative attitudes and thought patterns have changed yet.

F. As the Word changes the way you believe, speak, and expect things to be, you'll start experiencing your salvation benefits!

VI. Your whole outlook will change as you grow in the knowledge of God and His promises.

A. This is called "renewing your mind."

I beseech you therefore, brethren, by the mercies of God, that ye present your bodies a living sacrifice, holy, acceptable unto God, which is your reasonable service. And be not conformed to this world: but be ye transformed by the renewing of your mind, that ye may prove what is that good, and acceptable, and perfect, will of God.

ROMANS 12:1-2

B. The way you think must match your born-again spirit.

C. Your born-again spirit is always in agreement with God.

D. The Word will renew your mind to what's already happened in your spirit.

E. By submitting yourself to His Word, your life will change like a caterpillar transforming into a beautiful butterfly.

F. Be transformed by the knowledge of God, and your life will increasingly reflect Christ Jesus.

VII. Some people don't understand the spiritual nature of the radical change that occurred when they committed their lives to Christ.

A. They don't feel any different, and their circumstances certainly haven't changed.

B. Discouraged by this lack of immediate outward transformation, they incorrectly conclude that nothing really happened at salvation.

C. Because of this, many never go on to renew their minds and enjoy the benefits of salvation.

D. Your body and soul (mind, will, and emotions) didn't change at salvation the way your spirit did.

E. Your mind isn't instantly changed; it's your spirit that's been made new!

F. Since you can't see or touch your spirit, God's Word is the only way you can know what has happened within: **"It is the spirit that quickeneth; the flesh profiteth nothing: the words that I speak unto you, they are spirit, and they are life"** (John 6:63).

G. Faith is simply trusting what the Word says happened in your spirit more than what you see in the natural.

VIII. Feelings change, but the truth doesn't!

A. If you genuinely committed your life to the Lord, the truth is He will always honor that commitment.

B. Your relationship with God is secure.

C. Whether you felt anything or not, radical change took place in your spirit, and you're now a brand-new person—trust that God's Word to you is true!

D. You'll experience your salvation more as you renew your mind.

E. When you think according to the flesh (i.e., what your five senses tell you) and give in to negative external influences, you won't be able to enjoy God's benefits.

F. However, as you trust the truth of God's Word by keeping your mind on the Lord and thinking in line with your born-again spirit, you'll experience God's love, peace, joy, etc. (Gal. 5:22-23).

G. The choice is yours—begin renewing your mind today!

TEACHER'S
GUIDE

1. When God's Word first comes to you, Satan immediately tries to steal it (Matt. 13:19). However, he can only do so if you don't have understanding. That's why you need to comprehend what takes place the moment you accept the Lord. Understanding prevents the devil from talking you out of your salvation benefits.

   1a. According to Matthew 13:19, what does Satan immediately try to do when God's Word first comes to you?
   He tries to steal it from you
   1b. Understanding the Word prevents what?
   Satan talking you out of your salvation benefits

2. God's Word promises **"that if thou shalt confess with thy mouth the Lord Jesus, and shalt believe in thine heart that God hath raised him from the dead, thou shalt be saved. For with the heart man believeth unto righteousness; and with the mouth confession is made unto salvation"** (Rom. 10:9-10). **"For whosoever shall call upon the name of the Lord shall be saved"** (Rom. 10:13). Have you done this? If your answer is yes, then you've been saved! You were saved the very moment you sincerely committed your life to Jesus Christ. The truth of His Word instantly came to pass as you believed in your heart and confessed with your mouth.

   2a. God's Word promises in Romans 10:9 **"that if thou shalt confess with thy mouth the Lord Jesus, and shalt believe in thine heart that God hath raised him from the dead,"** you will be what?
   Saved
   2b. **"For _____ shall call upon the name of the Lord shall be saved"** (Rom. 10:13).
   "Whosoever"
   2c. True or false: You weren't saved until at least an hour after you sincerely committed your life to Jesus Christ.
   False

3. You're in good hands now! John 10:28-29 says,

> *I give unto them eternal life; and they shall never perish, neither shall any man pluck them out of my hand. My Father, which gave them me, is greater than all; and no man is able to pluck them out of my Father's hand.*

Since you've committed your life to Him, He'll keep you.

> *For the which cause I also suffer these things: nevertheless I am not ashamed: for I know whom I have believed, and am persuaded that he is able to keep that which I have committed unto him against that day.*
> 2 TIMOTHY 1:12

God will be faithful even when you aren't!

> *It is a faithful saying: For if we be dead with him, we shall also live with him: If we suffer, we shall also reign with him: if we deny him, he also will deny us: If we believe not, yet he abideth faithful: he cannot deny himself.*
> 2 TIMOTHY 2:11-13

When you make mistakes or feel discouraged, just remember—God can't deny Himself, because He always keeps His Word!

   3a. Since you've committed your life to Him, what will God do for you?
     He'll keep you
   3b. God will be _____ even when you aren't!
     Faithful

4. Knowledge from God's Word helps you comprehend what took place in your life at salvation. Knowing and following Him will bring you unspeakable joy. Salvation isn't just going to heaven when you die; God wants you to start experiencing your salvation benefits immediately. This requires knowledge from His Word. As you understand and act on that knowledge, you'll experience the benefits of your salvation.

   4a. How do you start experiencing the salvation benefits God has provided for you?
     By getting knowledge from His Word, and by understanding and acting on that knowledge

5. God has given you everything you need for life and godliness through the knowledge of Him.

> *Grace and peace be multiplied unto you through the knowledge of God,*
> *and of Jesus our Lord, According as his divine power hath given unto us*
> *all things that pertain unto life and godliness, through the knowledge of*
> *him that hath called us to glory and virtue: Whereby are given unto us*
> *exceeding great and precious promises: that by these ye might be partakers*
> *of the divine nature, having escaped the corruption that is in the world*
> *through lust.*
>
> 2 PETER 1:2-4

The knowledge of God gives you access to His promises. By believing and acting on them, you'll partake of His divine nature. This means you'll experience all of God's love, joy, peace, health, deliverance, prosperity, etc., that's already in your spirit now by Christ Jesus! As your thinking changes to line up with your born-again spirit, your life will change too. Just because you were born again doesn't mean that all of your negative attitudes and thought patterns have changed yet. As the Word changes the way you believe, speak, and expect things to be, you'll start experiencing your salvation benefits!

5a. According to 2 Peter 1:2-4, what has God given you through the knowledge of Him?
Everything you need for life and godliness
5b. As your thinking changes to line up with your born-again spirit, what will happen to your life?
It will change too
5c. True or false: As the Word changes the way you believe, speak, and expect things to be, you'll start experiencing salvation benefits.
True

6. Your whole outlook will change as you grow in the knowledge of God and His promises. This is called "renewing your mind."

> *I beseech you therefore, brethren, by the mercies of God, that ye present your bodies a living sacrifice, holy, acceptable unto God, which is your reasonable service. And be not conformed to this world: but be ye transformed by the renewing of your mind, that ye may prove what is that good, and acceptable, and perfect, will of God.*
>
> ROMANS 12:1-2

The way you think must match your born-again spirit. Your born-again spirit is always in agreement with God. The Word will renew your mind to what's already happened in your spirit. By submitting yourself to His Word, your life will change like a caterpillar transforming into a beautiful butterfly. Be transformed by the knowledge of God, and your life will increasingly reflect Christ Jesus.

6a. Your whole outlook will change as you grow in the knowledge of God and His promises—Romans 12:2 tells you this is called _____ _____ _____.
 <u>Renewing your mind</u>

6b. What must match your born-again spirit?
 A. Your furniture
 B. Your way of life
 C. Your thinking
 D. All of the above
 E. None of the above
 <u>C. Your thinking</u>

6c. Your life will increasingly reflect Jesus when you are what?
 <u>Transformed by the knowledge of God</u>

7. Some people don't understand the spiritual nature of the radical change that occurred when they committed their lives to Christ. They don't feel any different, and their circumstances certainly haven't changed. Discouraged by this lack of immediate outward transformation, they incorrectly conclude that nothing really happened at salvation. Because of this, many never go on to renew their minds and enjoy the benefits of salvation. Your body and soul (mind, will, and emotions) didn't change at salvation the way your spirit did. Your mind isn't instantly changed; it's your spirit that's been made new! Since you can't see or touch your spirit, God's Word is the only way you can know what has happened within: **"It is the spirit that quickeneth; the flesh profiteth nothing: the words that I speak unto you, they are spirit, and they are life"** (John 6:63). Faith is simply trusting what the Word says happened in your spirit more than what you see in the natural.

    7a. When people are discouraged by the lack of immediate outward transformation and conclude that nothing really happened at salvation, what do many never do?
        Go on to renew their minds and enjoy the benefits of salvation

    7b. Did your body and soul (mind, will, and emotions) change at salvation the same way your spirit did?
        No

    7c. Since you can't see or touch your spirit, what is the only way you can know what has happened within?
        God's Word

    7d. _____ is simply trusting what the Word says happened in your spirit more than what you see in the _____.
        Faith / natural

8. Feelings change, but the truth doesn't! If you genuinely committed your life to the Lord, the truth is He will always honor that commitment. Your relationship with God is secure. Whether you felt anything or not, radical change took place in your spirit, and you're now a brand-new person—trust that God's Word to you is true! You'll experience your salvation more as you renew your mind. When you think according to the flesh (i.e., what your five senses tell you) and give in to negative external influences, you won't be able to enjoy God's benefits. However, as you trust the truth of God's Word by keeping your mind on the Lord and thinking in line with your born-again spirit, you'll experience God's love, peace, joy, etc. (Gal. 5:22-23). The choice is yours—begin renewing your mind today!

8a. If you genuinely committed your life to the Lord, will He always honor that commitment?
Yes

8b. True or false: Your relationship with God is unstable.
False

8c. When you think according to the flesh (i.e., according to what your five senses tell you) and give in to negative external influences, what will you not be able to enjoy?
God's benefits

8d. How will you experience God's love, peace, joy, and all the other things listed in Galatians 5:22-23?
By trusting the truth of God's Word through keeping your mind on the Lord and thinking in line with your born-again spirit

8e. Is the choice yours to make?
Yes

DISCIPLESHIP
—— QUESTIONS ——

1. According to Matthew 13:19, what does Satan immediately try to do when God's Word first comes to you?

   _____
   _____
   _____

2. Understanding the Word prevents what?

   _____
   _____
   _____

3. God's Word promises in Romans 10:9 **"that if thou shalt confess with thy mouth the Lord Jesus, and shalt believe in thine heart that God hath raised him from the dead,"** you will be what?

   _____
   _____
   _____

4. **"For _____ shall call upon the name of the Lord shall be saved"** (Rom. 10:13).

5. True or false: You weren't saved until at least an hour after you sincerely committed your life to Jesus Christ.

6. Since you've committed your life to Him, what will God do for you?

   _____
   _____
   _____

7. God will be _____ even when you aren't!

8. How do you start experiencing the salvation benefits God has provided for you?

   _____
   _____
   _____

9. According to 2 Peter 1:2-4, what has God given you through the knowledge of Him?
    _____
    _____
    _____

10. As your thinking changes to line up with your born-again spirit, what will happen to your life?
    _____
    _____
    _____

11. True or false: As the Word changes the way you believe, speak, and expect things to be, you'll start experiencing salvation benefits.

12. Your whole outlook will change as you grow in the knowledge of God and His promises—Romans 12:2 tells you this is called _____ _____
    _____.

13. What must match your born-again spirit?
    A. Your furniture
    B. Your way of life
    C. Your thinking
    D. All of the above
    E. None of the above

14. Your life will increasingly reflect Jesus when you are what?
    _____
    _____
    _____

15. When people are discouraged by the lack of immediate outward transformation and conclude that nothing really happened at salvation, what do many never do?
    _____
    _____
    _____

16. Did your body and soul (mind, will, and emotions) change at salvation the same way your spirit did?
    _____
    _____
    _____

17. Since you can't see or touch your spirit, what is the only way you can know what has happened within?

_____

_____

_____

18. _____ is simply trusting what the Word says happened in your spirit more than what you see in the _____.

19. If you genuinely committed your life to the Lord, will He always honor that commitment?

_____

_____

_____

20. True or false: Your relationship with God is unstable.

21. When you think according to the flesh (i.e., according to what your five senses tell you) and give in to negative external influences, what will you not be able to enjoy?

_____

_____

_____

22. How will you experience God's love, peace, joy, and all the other things listed in Galatians 5:22-23?

_____

_____

_____

23. Is the choice yours to make?

_____

_____

_____

ANSWER
—KEY—

1. He tries to steal it from you

2. Satan talking you out of your salvation benefits

3. Saved

4. **"Whosoever"**

5. False

6. He'll keep you

7. Faithful

8. By getting knowledge from His Word, and by understanding and acting on that knowledge

9. Everything you need for life and godliness

10. It will change too

11. True

12. Renewing your mind

13. C. Your thinking

14. Transformed by the knowledge of God

15. Go on to renew their minds and enjoy the benefits of salvation

16. No

17. God's Word

18. Faith / natural

19. Yes

20. False

21. God's benefits

22. By trusting the truth of God's Word through keeping your mind on the Lord and thinking in line with your born-again spirit

23. Yes

—— SCRIPTURES ——

MATTHEW 13:19

When any one heareth the word of the kingdom, and understandeth it not, then cometh the wicked one, and catcheth away that which was sown in his heart. This is he which received seed by the way side.

ROMANS 10:9-10

That if thou shalt confess with thy mouth the Lord Jesus, and shalt believe in thine heart that God hath raised him from the dead, thou shalt be saved. [10] For with the heart man believeth unto righteousness; and with the mouth confession is made unto salvation.

ROMANS 10:13

For whosoever shall call upon the name of the Lord shall be saved.

JOHN 10:28-29

And I give unto them eternal life; and they shall never perish, neither shall any man pluck them out of my hand. [29] My Father, which gave them me, is greater than all; and no man is able to pluck them out of my Father's hand.

2 TIMOTHY 1:12

For the which cause I also suffer these things: nevertheless I am not ashamed: for I know whom I have believed, and am persuaded that he is able to keep that which I have committed unto him against that day.

2 TIMOTHY 2:11-13

It is a faithful saying: For if we be dead with him, we shall also live with him: [12] If we suffer, we shall also reign with him: if we deny him, he also will deny us: [13] If we believe not, yet he abideth faithful: he cannot deny himself.

2 PETER 1:2-4

Grace and peace be multiplied unto you through the knowledge of God, and of Jesus our Lord, [3] According as his divine power hath given unto us all things that pertain unto life and godliness, through the knowledge of him that hath called us to glory and virtue: [4] Whereby are given unto us exceeding great and precious promises: that by these ye might be partakers of the divine nature, having escaped the corruption that is in the world through lust.

ROMANS 12:1-2

I beseech you therefore, brethren, by the mercies of God, that ye present your bodies a living sacrifice, holy, acceptable unto God, which is your reasonable service. [2] And be not conformed to this world: but be ye transformed by the renewing of your mind, that ye may prove what is that good, and acceptable, and perfect, will of God.

2 CORINTHIANS 5:17

Therefore if any man be in Christ, he is a new creature: old things are passed away; behold, all things are become new.

JOHN 6:63

It is the spirit that quickeneth; the flesh profiteth nothing: the words that I speak unto you, they are spirit, and they are life.

MATTHEW 10:32

Whosoever therefore shall confess me before men, him will I confess also before my Father which is in heaven.

HEBREWS 13:5

Let your conversation be without covetousness; and be content with such things as ye have: for he hath said, I will never leave thee, nor forsake thee.

GALATIANS 5:22-23

But the fruit of the Spirit is love, joy, peace, longsuffering, gentleness, goodness, faith, [23] Meekness, temperance: against such there is no law.

JESUS
IS
LORD

Salvation is God's gift to you through faith in Jesus Christ. **"For the wages of sin is death; but the gift of God is eternal life through Jesus Christ our Lord"** (Rom. 6:23). Salvation can't be earned by any amount of good works, because God doesn't give eternal life based on anything you do. Jesus Christ did everything that needed to be done through His death, burial, and resurrection. You receive eternal life by faith in Him alone!

No one deserves to be saved because of their good works. **"For all have sinned, and come short of the glory of God"** (Rom. 3:23). God doesn't deal with you in proportion to your sin. If you miss heaven by an inch, then you've missed it by a mile. Either you are completely righteous in His sight or you're not. It's that simple! No matter how good you think you are, you've been bad enough to miss heaven!

The Lord explicitly stated that He's not just *a* way to the Father but *the* way! **"Jesus saith unto him, I am the way, the truth, and the life: no man cometh unto the Father, but by me"** (John 14:6). Acts 4:12 declares, **"Neither is there salvation in any other: for there is none other name under heaven given among men, whereby we must be saved."** Either you come to God the Father through faith in His Son Jesus Christ, or you don't come at all!

GOD IN THE FLESH

And when he was gone forth into the way, there came one running, and kneeled to him, and asked him, Good Master, what shall I do that I may inherit eternal life? And Jesus said unto him, Why callest thou me good? there is none good but one, that is, God. Thou knowest the commandments, Do not commit adultery, Do not kill, Do not steal, Do not bear false witness, Defraud not, Honour thy father and mother. And he answered and said unto him, Master, all these have I observed from my youth.

MARK 10:17-20

A rich young ruler asked Jesus, "What must I do to inherit eternal life?" He wanted to know how he could earn his way into heaven. Notice how the young man called Jesus **"Good Master"** at first. When the Lord countered him by saying that only God is good, he dropped **"Good"** and referred to Jesus simply as **"Master."** By this we know he didn't see Jesus as God.

Jesus Christ was God in the flesh. He wasn't just a good man who gave us a tremendous example of humility and love. He was literally God incarnate!

And without controversy great is the mystery of godliness: God was manifest in the flesh, justified in the Spirit, seen of angels, preached unto the Gentiles, believed on in the world, received up into glory.

1 TIMOTHY 3:16

Either Jesus was a deceiver, or He is who He said He was. No man who claimed to be God—but actually wasn't—should ever be considered "good." However, there's more verifiable historical evidence proving that Jesus Christ lived, died, **and** was resurrected than that Julius Caesar ever lived!

Every cult and religion on earth acknowledges Jesus's existence, but they stop short of calling Him God. They'll grant Him the status of a prophet or an inspired teacher sent from God but not Deity Himself. The rich young ruler did the same by dropping **"Good"** and simply calling Jesus **"Master."** He just couldn't bring himself to believe that this man standing before him was God.

Apart from Jesus being the Son of God, there's no way to the Father. Everything hinges on His divinity. The Lord Himself stated **"that all men should honour the Son, even as they honour the Father. He that honoureth not the Son honoureth not the Father which hath sent him"** (John 5:23). If Jesus wasn't God, then His life wasn't worth more than any other man's life, and He couldn't have atoned for the whole human race. However, since He was God in the flesh, His life was worth more than all mankind—making His sacrifice eternally sufficient for all!

THE GREAT EXCHANGE

Christianity is the only faith with a Savior. All other faiths depend on good works to achieve various degrees of "holiness." The holier you live, the better chance you have of being accepted by that "god." In essence, you become your own savior because "salvation" is based on your own performance. God knew you couldn't live a perfect life. Instead of demanding that you do everything right, He came and took your sin into His own body at the cross (1 Pet. 2:24). He suffered the punishment you deserved, to give you salvation as a gift. Praise God for the Savior!

Jesus took your sin so you could become righteous. **"For he hath made him to be sin for us, who knew no sin; that we might be made the righteousness of God in him"** (2 Cor. 5:21). God put His judgment for sin upon Christ at the cross so that you wouldn't have to bear it. Then, when you believed and received the Lord, He placed Jesus's righteousness on you. This is the Great Exchange!

When this exchange takes place, your spirit is immediately recreated with the righteousness of Jesus Christ. You are then able to fellowship with God spirit to Spirit. **"God is a Spirit: and they that worship him must worship him in spirit and in truth"** (John 4:24). Even when you sin, your born-again spirit cannot be contaminated, because of the impenetrable seal of Christ's own Spirit:

> *In whom ye also trusted, after that ye heard the word of truth, the gospel of*
> *your salvation: in whom also after that ye believed, ye were sealed with that*
> *holy Spirit of promise.*
>
> EPHESIANS 1:13

Since the new nature of your spirit is always holy, you can approach God at any time and in any condition. Now, that's good news!

SUSTAINED BY FAITH

The Christian life is both born in faith and sustained by faith. You'll just end up condemning yourself if you try to live it by your own works. As long as you're in your physical body, there'll be times when you fall short. If you're not careful, you'll beat yourself up trying to live right, and wonder how God could ever love someone who messes up as much as you.

God's love doesn't change when you make mistakes. If He went to the cross for you as a sinner, how much more does He love you now that you're a Christian!

> *But God commendeth his love toward us, in that, while we were yet sinners, Christ died for us. Much more then, being now justified by his blood, we shall be saved from wrath through him. For if, when we were enemies, we were reconciled to God by the death of his Son, much more, being reconciled, we shall be saved by his life.*
> ROMANS 5:8-10

He loves you more now as a Christian—even when you sin—than He did when you were lost. Don't ever let your failures separate you from God's unfailing love!

THE LAW'S PURPOSE

God gave the Law to show man he couldn't save himself. The Ten Commandments are really just the tip of the iceberg; there are literally thousands of rules to keep in the Law! Jesus used several of these commandments in an attempt to show the rich young ruler we read about in Mark 10 that he would never be holy enough for eternal life on his own: **"Thou knowest the commandments, Do not commit adultery, Do not kill, Do not steal, Do not bear false witness, Defraud not, Honour thy father and mother"** (Mark 10:19). This young man genuinely thought he could do something to earn eternal life. Doing and receiving by faith are very different from each other indeed!

The Law is like a plate glass window. Whether you break it with a BB or a boulder, it's broken! **"For whosoever shall keep the whole law, and yet offend in one point, he is guilty of all"** (James 2:10). God doesn't tell you to do your best and He'll make up the difference with mercy. Either you live holy and receive eternal life because you earned it (which is not possible), or you receive it by faith as a gift.

This deceived young ruler needed to quit trying and start trusting. In an effort to convince the Lord that he deserved eternal life, he told Jesus that he'd kept all of the commandments since his youth. Impossible! This man's attitude had him going straight to hell!

Loving the young ruler, Jesus tried to bring him out of this deception.

> *Then Jesus beholding him loved him, and said unto him, One thing thou lackest: go thy way, sell whatsoever thou hast, and give to the poor, and thou shalt have treasure in heaven: and come, take up the cross, and follow me. And he was sad at that saying, and went away grieved: for he had great possessions.*
> MARK 10:21-22

The Lord touched this man's true "god" when He instructed him to sell all of his possessions and give to the poor. The rich young ruler wasn't willing to lay them down and make Jesus Lord, because he'd broken the very first command: **"Thou shalt have no other gods before me"** (Ex. 20:3).

God is not against you having money, but He's against money having you! Giving away all of your possessions to the poor is not a requirement for salvation. When Zacchaeus, another wealthy man, met Jesus and repented, he declared he'd give half of all he had to the poor (Luke 19:1-9). Jesus never asked this of him, but Zacchaeus volunteered to do it because his heart had changed. The issue Jesus is driving at is who or what do you trust in as your "god"/God?

THE BOTTOM LINE

If you believe that Jesus Christ was only a good person and that you can get to God through many different ways, you haven't truly made Him Lord of your life. Jesus is either Lord of all, or He isn't Lord at all! You can't receive salvation, which comes only through Him, if you aren't willing to bow your knee and acknowledge Him as God and Supreme Ruler. Either Jesus Christ is your Savior **and** Lord, or He's not. It's that simple!

— OUTLINE —

I. Salvation is God's gift to you through faith in Jesus Christ.

    A. **"For the wages of sin is death; but the gift of God is eternal life through Jesus Christ our Lord"** (Rom. 6:23).

    B. Salvation can't be earned by any amount of good works, because God doesn't give eternal life based on anything you do.

    C. Jesus Christ did everything that needed to be done through His death, burial, and resurrection.

    D. No one deserves to be saved because of their good works—**"For all have sinned, and come short of the glory of God"** (Rom. 3:23).

    E. Either you are completely righteous in His sight or you're not.

    F. The Lord explicitly stated that He's not just *a* way to the Father but *the* way—**"Jesus saith unto him, I am the way, the truth, and the life: no man cometh unto the Father, but by me"** (John 14:6).

    G. Either you come to God the Father through faith in His Son Jesus Christ, or you don't come at all!

II. Jesus Christ was God in the flesh.

    A. He wasn't just a good man who gave us a tremendous example of humility and love— He was literally God incarnate!

    And without controversy great is the mystery of godliness: God was manifest in the flesh, justified in the Spirit, seen of angels, preached unto the Gentiles, believed on in the world, received up into glory.

                                 1 TIMOTHY 3:16

    B. Either Jesus was a deceiver, or He is who He said He was.

    C. Every cult and religion on earth acknowledges Jesus's existence, but they stop short of calling Him God.

    D. They'll grant Him the status of a prophet or an inspired teacher sent from God but not Deity Himself.

    E. Everything hinges on Jesus's divinity.

    F. If Jesus wasn't God, then His life wasn't worth more than any other man's life, and He couldn't have atoned for the whole human race.

G. However, since He was God in the flesh, His life was worth more than all mankind—making His sacrifice eternally sufficient for all!

III. Christianity is the only faith with a Savior.

A. All other faiths depend on good works to achieve various degrees of "holiness."

B. In essence, you become your own savior because "salvation" is based on your own performance.

C. God knew you couldn't live a perfect life.

D. Instead of demanding that you do everything right, He came and took your sin into His own body at the cross (1 Pet. 2:24).

E. He suffered the punishment you deserved, to give you salvation as a gift.

F. **"For he hath made him to be sin for us, who knew no sin; that we might be made the righteousness of God in him"** (2 Cor. 5:21).

G. When this exchange takes place, your spirit is immediately recreated with the righteousness of Jesus Christ.

H. You are then able to fellowship with God spirit to Spirit—**"God is a Spirit: and they that worship him must worship him in spirit and in truth"** (John 4:24).

I. Even when you sin, your born-again spirit cannot be contaminated, because of the impenetrable seal of Christ's own Spirit:

In whom ye also trusted, after that ye heard the word of truth, the gospel of your salvation: in whom also after that ye believed, ye were sealed with that holy Spirit of promise.

EPHESIANS 1:13

J. Since the new nature of your spirit is always holy, you can approach God at any time and in any condition.

IV. The Christian life is both born in faith and sustained by faith.

A. You'll just end up condemning yourself if you try to live it by your own works.

B. As long as you're in your physical body, there'll be times when you fall short.

C. God's love doesn't change when you make mistakes.

D. If He went to the cross for you as a sinner, how much more does He love you now that you're a Christian!

But God commendeth his love toward us, in that, while we were yet sinners, Christ died for us. Much more then, being now justified by his blood, we shall be saved from wrath through him. For if, when we were enemies, we were reconciled to God by the death of his Son, much more, being reconciled, we shall be saved by his life.

ROMANS 5:8-10

E. He loves you more now as a Christian—even when you sin—than He did when you were lost.

F. Don't ever let your failures separate you from God's unfailing love!

V. God gave the Law to show man he couldn't save himself.

A. Jesus used several of these commandments in an attempt to show the rich young ruler we read about in Mark 10 that he would never be holy enough for eternal life on his own.

B. This young man genuinely thought he could do something to earn eternal life.

C. Doing and receiving by faith are very different from each other indeed!

D. The Law is like a plate glass window—whether you break it with a BB or a boulder, it's broken!

E. **"For whosoever shall keep the whole law, and yet offend in one point, he is guilty of all"** (James 2:10).

F. Either you live holy and receive eternal life because you earned it (which is not possible), or you receive it by faith as a gift.

G. Who or what do you trust in as your "god"/God?

VI. If you believe Jesus Christ was only a good person and that you can get to God through many different ways, you haven't truly made Him Lord of your life.

A. Jesus is either Lord of all, or He isn't Lord at all!

B. Either Jesus Christ is your Savior **and** Lord, or He's not—it's that simple!

TEACHER'S GUIDE

1. Salvation is God's gift to you through faith in Jesus Christ. **"For the wages of sin is death; but the gift of God is eternal life through Jesus Christ our Lord"** (Rom. 6:23). Salvation can't be earned by any amount of good works, because God doesn't give eternal life based on anything you do. Jesus Christ did everything that needed to be done through His death, burial, and resurrection. No one deserves to be saved because of their good works—**"For all have sinned, and come short of the glory of God"** (Rom. 3:23). Either you are completely righteous in His sight or you're not. The Lord explicitly stated that He's not just *a* way to the Father but *the* way—**"Jesus saith unto him, I am the way, the truth, and the life: no man cometh unto the Father, but by me"** (John 14:6). Either you come to God the Father through faith in His Son Jesus Christ, or you don't come at all!

    1a. Romans 6:23 says, **"For the wages of sin is death; but the gift of God is** _____ _____ **through Jesus Christ our Lord."**
        <u>**"Eternal life"**</u>

    1b. Why can't salvation be earned by any amount of good works?
        <u>**Because God doesn't give eternal life based on anything you do**</u>

    1c. True or false: Jesus Christ did most of what needs to be done through His death, burial, and resurrection.
        <u>**False**</u>

    1d. According to John 14:6, can you come to God through some way other than Jesus?
        <u>**No**</u>

2. Jesus Christ was God in the flesh. He wasn't just a good man who gave us a tremendous example of humility and love—He was literally God incarnate!

> *And without controversy great is the mystery of godliness: God was manifest in the flesh, justified in the Spirit, seen of angels, preached unto the Gentiles, believed on in the world, received up into glory.*
>
> 1 TIMOTHY 3:16

Either Jesus was a deceiver, or He is who He said He was. Every cult and religion on earth acknowledges Jesus's existence, but they stop short of calling Him God. They'll grant Him the status of a prophet or an inspired teacher sent from God but not Deity Himself. Everything hinges on Jesus's divinity. If Jesus wasn't God, then His life wasn't worth more than any other man's life, and He couldn't have atoned for the whole human race. However, since He was God in the flesh, His life was worth more than all mankind—making His sacrifice eternally sufficient for all!

    2a. According to 1 Timothy 3:16, Jesus was literally…
       A. God incarnate
       B. A wise prophet
       C. A good man
       D. All of the above
       E. None of the above
       A. God incarnate
    2b. How could Jesus atone for the whole human race?
       He was God in the flesh, so His life was worth more than all mankind, making His sacrifice eternally sufficient for all

3. Christianity is the only faith with a Savior. All other faiths depend on good works to achieve various degrees of "holiness." In essence, you become your own savior because "salvation" is based on your own performance. God knew you couldn't live a perfect life. Instead of demanding that you do everything right, He came and took your sin into His own body at the cross (1 Pet. 2:24). He suffered the punishment you deserved, to give you salvation as a gift. **"For he hath made him to be sin for us, who knew no sin; that we might be made the righteousness of God in him"** (2 Cor. 5:21). When this exchange takes place, your spirit is immediately recreated with the righteousness of Jesus Christ. You are then able to fellowship with God spirit to Spirit—**"God is a Spirit: and they that worship him must worship him in spirit and in truth"** (John 4:24). Even when you sin, your born-again spirit cannot be contaminated, because of the impenetrable seal of Christ's own Spirit:

> *In whom ye also trusted, after that ye heard the word of truth, the gospel of your salvation: in whom also after that ye believed, ye were sealed with that holy Spirit of promise.*
>
> EPHESIANS 1:13

Since the new nature of your spirit is always holy, you can approach God at any time and in any condition.

   3a. Christianity is the only faith with a _____.
      Savior
   3b. In all other faiths, why do you, in essence, become your own savior?
      Because "salvation" is based on your own performance
   3c. True or false: You can live a perfect life.
      False
   3d. **"For he hath made him to be sin for us, who knew no sin; that we might be made the"** what, according to 2 Corinthians 5:21?
      "Righteousness of God in him"
   3e. Which scripture tells you that **"ye were sealed with that holy Spirit of promise"**?
      Ephesians 1:13
   3f. Since the new nature of your spirit is always holy, can you approach God at any time and in any condition?
      Yes

4. The Christian life is both born in faith and sustained by faith. You'll just end up condemning yourself if you try to live it by your own works. As long as you're in your physical body, there'll be times when you fall short. God's love doesn't change when you make mistakes. If He went to the cross for you as a sinner, how much more does He love you now that you're a Christian!

> *But God commendeth his love toward us, in that, while we were yet sinners, Christ died for us. Much more then, being now justified by his blood, we shall be saved from wrath through him. For if, when we were enemies, we were reconciled to God by the death of his Son, much more, being reconciled, we shall be saved by his life.*
>
> ROMANS 5:8-10

He loves you more now as a Christian—even when you sin—than He did when you were lost. Don't ever let your failures separate you from God's unfailing love!

4a. Since the Christian life is both born in faith and sustained by faith, what will happen if you try to live it by your own works?
You'll end up condemning yourself

4b. As long as you're in your physical body, there'll be times when you what?
A. Do the hokey pokey
B. Make mistakes
C. Get everything perfectly and consistently right
D. All of the above
E. None of the above
B. Make mistakes

4c. God's _____ doesn't _____ when you make mistakes.
Love / change

4d. What does Romans 5:8-10 tell you happened while you were yet a sinner?
Christ died for you

4e. True or false: You should let your failures separate you from God's love.
False

5. God gave the Law to show man he couldn't save himself. Jesus used several of these commandments in an attempt to show the rich young ruler we read about in Mark 10 that he would never be holy enough for eternal life on his own. This young man genuinely thought he could do something to earn eternal life. Doing and receiving by faith are very different from each other indeed! The Law is like a plate glass window—whether you break it with a BB or a boulder, it's broken! **"For whosoever shall keep the whole law, and yet offend in one point, he is guilty of all"** (James 2:10). Either you live holy and receive eternal life because you earned it (which is not possible), or you receive it by faith as a gift. Who or what do you trust in as your "god"/God?

    5a. Why did God give the Law?
       To show man that he couldn't save himself

    5b. Are doing and receiving by faith the same thing?
       No

    5c. James 2:10 says, **"For whosoever shall keep the whole law, and yet offend in one point, he is _____ of all."**
       "Guilty"

6. If you believe that Jesus Christ was only a good person and that you can get to God through many different ways, you haven't truly made Him Lord of your life. Jesus is either Lord of all, or He isn't Lord at all! Either Jesus Christ is your Savior **and** Lord, or He's not—it's that simple!

    6a. If you believe that Jesus Christ was only a good person and that you can get to God through many different ways, what haven't you done?
       Truly made Him Lord of your life

DISCIPLESHIP
—— QUESTIONS ——

1. Romans 6:23 says, **"For the wages of sin is death; but the gift of God is
   _____ _____through Jesus Christ our Lord."**

2. Why can't salvation be earned by any amount of good works?
   _____
   _____
   _____

3. True or false: Jesus Christ did most of what needs to be done through His death, burial, and resurrection.

4. According to John 14:6, can you come to God through some way other than Jesus?
   _____
   _____
   _____

5. According to 1 Timothy 3:16, Jesus was literally...
   A. God incarnate
   B. A wise prophet
   C. A good man
   D. All of the above
   E. None of the above

6. How could Jesus atone for the whole human race?
   _____
   _____
   _____

7. Christianity is the only faith with a _____.

8. In all other faiths, why do you, in essence, become your own savior?
   _____
   _____
   _____

9. True or false: You can live a perfect life.

10. **"For he hath made him to be sin for us, who knew no sin; that we might be made the"** what, according to 2 Corinthians 5:21?

_____

_____

_____

11. Which scripture tells you that **"ye were sealed with that holy Spirit of promise"**?

_____

_____

_____

12. Since the new nature of your spirit is always holy, can you approach God at any time and in any condition?

_____

_____

_____

13. Since the Christian life is both born in faith and sustained by faith, what will happen if you try to live it by your own works?

_____

_____

_____

14. As long as you're in your physical body, there'll be times when you what?
    A. Do the hokey pokey
    B. Make mistakes
    C. Get everything perfectly and consistently right
    D. All of the above
    E. None of the above

15. God's _____ doesn't _____ when you make mistakes.

16. What does Romans 5:8-10 tell you happened while you were yet a sinner?

_____

_____

_____

17. True or false: You should let your failures separate you from God's love.

18. Why did God give the Law?

_____

_____

_____

19. Are doing and receiving by faith the same thing?

20. James 2:10 says, **"For whosoever shall keep the whole law, and yet offend in one point, he is _____ of all."**

21. If you believe that Jesus Christ was only a good person and that you can get to God through many different ways, what haven't you done?

ANSWER
—KEY—

1. **"Eternal life"**

2. Because God doesn't give eternal life based on anything you do

3. False

4. No

5. A. God incarnate

6. He was God in the flesh, so His life was worth more than all mankind, making His sacrifice eternally sufficient for all

7. Savior

8. Because "salvation" is based on your own performance

9. False

10. **"Righteousness of God in him"**

11. Ephesians 1:13

12. Yes

13. You'll end up condemning yourself

14. B. Make mistakes

15. Love / change

16. Christ died for you

17. False

18. To show man that he couldn't save himself

19. No

20. **"Guilty"**

21. Truly made Him Lord of your life

—— SCRIPTURES ——

ROMANS 6:23

For the wages of sin is death; but the gift of God is eternal life through Jesus Christ our Lord.

ROMANS 3:23

For all have sinned, and come short of the glory of God.

JOHN 14:6

Jesus saith unto him, I am the way, the truth, and the life: no man cometh unto the Father, but by me.

ACTS 4:12

Neither is there salvation in any other: for there is none other name under heaven given among men, whereby we must be saved.

MARK 10:17-22

And when he was gone forth into the way, there came one running, and kneeled to him, and asked him, Good Master, what shall I do that I may inherit eternal life? [18] And Jesus said unto him, Why callest thou me good? there is none good but one, that is, God. [19] Thou knowest the commandments, Do not commit adultery, Do not kill, Do not steal, Do not bear false witness, Defraud not, Honour thy father and mother. [20] And he answered and said unto him, Master, all these have I observed from my youth. [21] Then Jesus beholding him loved him, and said unto him, One thing thou lackest: go thy way, sell whatsoever thou hast, and give to the poor, and thou shalt have treasure in heaven: and come, take up the cross, and follow me. [22] And he was sad at that saying, and went away grieved: for he had great possessions.

1 TIMOTHY 3:16

And without controversy great is the mystery of godliness: God was manifest in the flesh, justified in the Spirit, seen of angels, preached unto the Gentiles, believed on in the world, received up into glory.

JOHN 5:23

That all men should honour the Son, even as they honour the Father. He that honoureth not the Son honoureth not the Father which hath sent him.

1 PETER 2:24

Who his own self bare our sins in his own body on the tree, that we, being dead to sins, should live unto righteousness: by whose stripes ye were healed.

2 CORINTHIANS 5:21

For he hath made him to be sin for us, who knew no sin; that we might be made the righteousness of God in him.

JOHN 4:24

God is a Spirit: and they that worship him must worship him in spirit and in truth.

EPHESIANS 1:13

In whom ye also trusted, after that ye heard the word of truth, the gospel of your salvation: in whom also after that ye believed, ye were sealed with that holy Spirit of promise.

ROMANS 5:8-10

But God commendeth his love toward us, in that, while we were yet sinners, Christ died for us. [9] Much more then, being now justified by his blood, we shall be saved from wrath through him. [10] For if, when we were enemies, we were reconciled to God by the death of his Son, much more, being reconciled, we shall be saved by his life.

JAMES 2:10

For whosoever shall keep the whole law, and yet offend in one point, he is guilty of all.

EXODUS 20:3

Thou shalt have no other gods before me.

LUKE 19:1-9

And Jesus entered and passed through Jericho. [2] And, behold, there was a man named Zacchaeus, which was the chief among the publicans, and he was rich. [3] And he sought to see Jesus who he was; and could not for the press, because he was little of stature. [4] And he ran before, and climbed up into a sycomore tree to see him: for he was to pass that way. [5] And when Jesus came to the place, he looked up, and saw him, and said unto him, Zacchaeus, make haste, and come down; for to day I must abide at thy house. [6] And he made haste, and came down, and received him joyfully. [7] And when they saw it, they all murmured, saying, That he was gone to be guest with a man that is a sinner. [8] And Zacchaeus stood, and said unto the Lord; Behold, Lord, the half of my goods I give to the poor; and if I have taken any thing from any man by false accusation, I restore him fourfold. [9] And Jesus said unto him, This day is salvation come to this house, forsomuch as he also is a son of Abraham.

FROM
DEATH
TO
LIFE

All people are born into this world separated from God (Ps. 51:5). Adam and Eve died spiritually when they sinned. Even though they didn't die physically right away, their spirits were separated from God and fell under the control of Satan (Gen. 3). Every person born into the earth since then has had this inherent sin nature. **"Wherefore, as by one man sin entered into the world, and death by sin; and so death passed upon all men, for that all have sinned"** (Rom. 5:12).

However, sin isn't imputed until you reach the age of accountability. This means you aren't held responsible for your sin until you're old enough to intentionally violate God's Law (Rom. 7:9). This age varies from person to person, but you need to be born again as soon as possible once you reach it.

A natural birth brought you into this world, but a spiritual birth is required to enter God's kingdom.

> *Jesus answered and said unto him, Verily, verily, I say unto thee, Except a man be born again, he cannot see the kingdom of God. Nicodemus saith unto him, How can a man be born when he is old? can he enter the second time into his mother's womb, and be born? Jesus answered, Verily, verily, I say unto thee, Except a man be born of water and of the Spirit, he cannot enter into the kingdom of God.*
>
> JOHN 3:3-5

When you're born again, you pass from death to life. **"Verily, verily, I say unto you, He that heareth my word, and believeth on him that sent me, hath everlasting life, and shall not come into condemnation; but is passed from death unto life"** (John 5:24). At salvation, the sin nature you were born with dies and is replaced with a brand-new, righteous nature. You're no longer a sinner but righteous in Christ!

NEVER AGAIN!

God's standard of goodness is His own glory. We might have looked good compared to other sinners, but no one is holy compared to Jesus. According to Romans 3:23, **"all have sinned, and come short of the glory of God."** Who wants to be the best sinner who ever went to hell? We all need a Savior. God declared everyone a sinner, but He loved us and wanted to redeem us. And in doing so, He could declare everyone righteous who has accepted Jesus by faith. Regardless of how bad we were, we instantly became righteous through receiving Christ.

Born-again Christians know they don't deserve salvation based on their own merits. It's only because they put faith in Jesus Christ and His finished work on the cross. All other religions try to approach God based on their personal holiness—what they do for Him. Christians approach God based on a firm heart belief in what He did for them.

All of your sins were forgiven—past, present, and future—the moment you received the Lord. You are now eternally redeemed and have an eternal inheritance (Heb. 9-10). In your spirit, you became sanctified and perfected in God's sight forever. **"To the general assembly and church of the firstborn, which are written in heaven, and to God the Judge of all, and to the spirits of just men made perfect"** (Heb. 12:23). Sin will never be imputed to you (credited to your account) again!

CHOOSE LIFE!

Even though you're completely forgiven, it matters how you live! You have an Enemy who is committed to your destruction.

> *The thief cometh not, but for to steal, and to kill, and to destroy: I am come*
> *that they might have life, and that they might have it more abundantly.*
> JOHN 10:10

The choices you make determine whether you experience life or death. **"Know ye not, that to whom ye yield yourselves servants to obey, his servants ye are to whom ye obey; whether of sin unto death, or of obedience unto righteousness?"** (Rom. 6:16). Yield to sin and you're yielding to the one whose revealed purpose is to steal, kill, and destroy you. Sin gives the devil a foothold in your life, and he'll take full advantage of it!

If you sin, simply repent. God will never leave you nor forsake you. He's already forgiven you, so don't fall for the deception that He doesn't love you or that you'll lose your salvation. God the Father already rejected and judged Jesus so you wouldn't have to be rejected and judged. Change your mind and turn from the sin. Declare, "Satan, I rebuke you. The blood of Jesus has set me free. Even though I didn't do what was right, you cannot destroy me. God loves me and I choose to follow Him!" This prevents Satan from gaining entrance into your life.

Don't let the devil take advantage of you by you ignoring the way God shows you to live. Renew your mind to His Word and act on it in faith. The abundant life Jesus provided is yours to enjoy!

For Further Information:

For further study, I recommend my teaching *Spirit, Soul & Body*.

—— OUTLINE ——

I. All people are born into this world separated from God (Ps. 51:5).

    A. Adam and Eve died spiritually when they sinned.

    B. Even though they didn't die physically right away, their spirits were separated from God and fell under the control of Satan (Gen. 3).

    C. Every person born into the earth since then has had this inherent sin nature.

    D. **"Wherefore, as by one man sin entered into the world, and death by sin; and so death passed upon all men, for that all have sinned"** (Rom. 5:12).

    E. A natural birth brought you into this world, but a spiritual birth is required to enter God's kingdom.

> *Jesus answered and said unto him, Verily, verily, I say unto thee, Except a man be born again, he cannot see the kingdom of God. Nicodemus saith unto him, How can a man be born when he is old? can he enter the second time into his mother's womb, and be born? Jesus answered, Verily, verily, I say unto thee, Except a man be born of water and of the Spirit, he cannot enter into the kingdom of God.*
>
> JOHN 3:3-5

    F. When you're born again, you pass from death to life—**"Verily, verily, I say unto you, He that heareth my word, and believeth on him that sent me, hath everlasting life, and shall not come into condemnation; but is passed from death unto life"** (John 5:24).

    G. You're no longer a sinner but righteous in Christ!

II. God's standard of goodness is His own glory.

    A. You might have looked good compared to other sinners, but no one is holy compared to Jesus.

    B. According to Romans 3:23, **"all have sinned, and come short of the glory of God."**

    C. God declared everyone a sinner, but He loved you and wanted to redeem you.

    D. Regardless of how bad you were, you instantly became righteous through receiving Christ.

    E. All of your sins were forgiven—past, present, and future—the moment you received the Lord.

    F. You are now eternally redeemed and have an eternal inheritance (Heb. 9-10).

G. In your spirit, you became sanctified and perfected in God's sight forever—**"To the general assembly and church of the firstborn, which are written in heaven, and to God the Judge of all, and to the spirits of just men made perfect"** (Heb. 12:23).

H. Sin will never be imputed to you (credited to your account) again!

III. Even though you're completely forgiven, it matters how you live!

A. You have an Enemy who is committed to your destruction.

> *The thief cometh not, but for to steal, and to kill, and to destroy: I am come that they might have life, and that they might have it more abundantly.*
>
> JOHN 10:10

B. The choices you make determine whether you experience life or death.

C. **"Know ye not, that to whom ye yield yourselves servants to obey, his servants ye are to whom ye obey; whether of sin unto death, or of obedience unto righteousness?"** (Rom. 6:16).

D. Yield to sin and you're yielding to the one whose revealed purpose is to steal, kill, and destroy you.

E. If you sin, simply repent.

F. God has already forgiven you, so don't fall for the deception that He doesn't love you or that you'll lose your salvation.

G. God the Father already rejected and judged Jesus so you wouldn't have to be rejected and judged.

H. Change your mind and turn from the sin—declare, "Satan, I rebuke you. The blood of Jesus has set me free. Even though I didn't do what was right, you cannot destroy me. God loves me and I choose to follow Him!"

I. This prevents Satan from gaining entrance into your life.

J. Don't let the devil take advantage of you by you ignoring the way God shows you to live.

K. The abundant life Jesus provided is yours to enjoy!

TEACHER'S
GUIDE

1. All people are born into this world separated from God (Ps. 51:5). Adam and Eve died spiritually when they sinned. Even though they didn't die physically right away, their spirits were separated from God and fell under the control of Satan (Gen. 3). Every person born into the earth since then has had this inherent sin nature. **"Wherefore, as by one man sin entered into the world, and death by sin; and so death passed upon all men, for that all have sinned"** (Rom. 5:12). A natural birth brought you into this world, but a spiritual birth is required to enter God's kingdom.

> *Jesus answered and said unto him, Verily, verily, I say unto thee, Except a man be born again, he cannot see the kingdom of God. Nicodemus saith unto him, How can a man be born when he is old? can he enter the second time into his mother's womb, and be born? Jesus answered, Verily, verily, I say unto thee, Except a man be born of water and of the Spirit, he cannot enter into the kingdom of God.*
>
> JOHN 3:3-5

When you're born again, you pass from death to life—**"Verily, verily, I say unto you, He that heareth my word, and believeth on him that sent me, hath everlasting life, and shall not come into condemnation; but is passed from death unto life"** (John 5:24). You're no longer a sinner but righteous in Christ!

1a. How are all people born into this world?
   A. Perfect
   B. Ready for anything
   C. Separated from God
   D. All of the above
   E. None of the above
   C. Separated from God
1b. Romans 5:12 says, **"Wherefore, as by one man sin entered into the world, and death by sin; and so death passed upon _____ men, for that _____ have sinned."**
   "All" / "all"
1c. What is required to enter God's kingdom?
   A. spiritual birth
1d. According to John 5:24, what happens to you when you're born again?
   You pass from death to life

2. God's standard of goodness is His own glory. You might have looked good compared to other sinners, but no one is holy compared to Jesus. According to Romans 3:23, **"all have sinned, and come short of the glory of God."** God declared everyone a sinner, but He loved you and wanted to redeem you. Regardless of how bad you were, you instantly became righteous through receiving Christ. All of your sins were forgiven—past, present, and future—the moment you received the Lord. You are now eternally redeemed and have an eternal inheritance (Heb. 9-10). In your spirit, you became sanctified and perfected in God's sight forever—**"To the general assembly and church of the firstborn, which are written in heaven, and to God the Judge of all, and to the spirits of just men made perfect"** (Heb. 12:23). Sin will never be imputed to you (credited to your account) again!

    2a. True or false: God's standard of goodness is His own glory.
        True
    2b. What does Romans 3:23 tell you?
        That you might have looked good compared to other sinners, but no one is holy
        compared to Jesus, because "all have sinned, and come short of the glory of God"
    2c. Did God want to redeem you?
        Yes
    2d. In your spirit, you became _____ and _____ in God's sight forever.
        Sanctified / perfected
    2e. Will sin ever be imputed to you (credited to your account) again?
        No

3. Even though you're completely forgiven, it matters how you live! You have an Enemy who is committed to your destruction.

> *The thief cometh not, but for to steal, and to kill, and to destroy: I am come that they might have life, and that they might have it more abundantly.*
> JOHN 10:10

The choices you make determine whether you experience life or death. **"Know ye not, that to whom ye yield yourselves servants to obey, his servants ye are to whom ye obey; whether of sin unto death, or of obedience unto righteousness?"** (Rom. 6:16). Yield to sin and you're yielding to the one whose revealed purpose is to steal, kill, and destroy you. If you sin, simply repent. God has already forgiven you, so don't fall for the deception that He doesn't love you or that you'll lose your salvation. God the Father already rejected and judged Jesus so you wouldn't have to be rejected and judged. Change your mind and turn from the sin—declare, "Satan, I rebuke you. The blood of Jesus has set me free. Even though I didn't do what was right, you cannot destroy me. God loves me and I choose to follow Him!" This prevents Satan from gaining entrance into your life. Don't let the devil take advantage of you by you ignoring the way God shows you to live. The abundant life Jesus provided is yours to enjoy!

3a. True or false: You have an Enemy who is committed to your destruction.
True

3b. **"Know ye not, that to whom ye** _____ **yourselves servants to** _____**, his servants ye are to whom ye obey; whether of sin unto death, or of obedience unto righteousness?"** (Rom. 6:16).
A. Give / sing
B. Make / stand
C. Submit / listen
D. All of the above
E. None of the above
E. None of the above

3c. If you yield to sin, what are you doing?
You are yielding yourself to the one whose revealed purpose is to steal, kill, and destroy you

3d. What did God the Father do so that you wouldn't have to be rejected and judged?
Reject and judge Jesus

3e. Can the devil take advantage of you if you ignore the way God shows you to live?
Yes

DISCIPLESHIP
—— QUESTIONS ——

1. How are all people born into this world?
    A. Perfect
    B. Ready for anything
    C. Separated from God
    D. All of the above
    E. None of the above

2. Romans 5:12 says, **"Wherefore, as by one man sin entered into the world, and death by sin; and so death passed upon _____ men, for that _____ have sinned."**

3. What is required to enter God's kingdom?
    _____
    _____
    _____

4. According to John 5:24, what happens to you when you're born again?
    _____
    _____
    _____

5. True or false: God's standard of goodness is His own glory.

6. What does Romans 3:23 tell you?
    _____
    _____
    _____

7. Did God want to redeem you?
    _____
    _____
    _____

8. In your spirit, you became _____ and _____ in God's sight forever.

9. Will sin ever be imputed to you (credited to your account) again?

_____

_____

_____

10. True or false: You have an Enemy who is committed to your destruction.

11. **"Know ye not, that to whom ye _____ yourselves servants to _____, his servants ye are to whom ye obey; whether of sin unto death, or of obedience unto righteousness?"** (Rom. 6:16).
    A. Give / sing
    B. Make / stand
    C. Submit / listen
    D. All of the above
    E. None of the above

12. If you yield to sin, what are you doing?

_____

_____

_____

13. What did God the Father do so that you wouldn't have to be rejected and judged?

_____

_____

_____

14. Can the devil take advantage of you if you ignore the way God shows you to live?

_____

_____

_____

ANSWER
—KEY—

1. C. Separated from God

2. **"All" / "all"**

3. A spiritual birth

4. You pass from death to life

5. True

6. That you might have looked good compared to other sinners, but no one is holy compared to Jesus, because **"all have sinned, and come short of the glory of God"**

7. Yes

8. Sanctified / perfected

9. No

10. True

11. E. None of the above

12. You are yielding yourself to the one whose revealed purpose is to steal, kill, and destroy you

13. Reject and judge Jesus

14. Yes

—— SCRIPTURES——

PSALM 51:5

Behold, I was shapen in iniquity; and in sin did my mother conceive me.

ROMANS 5:12

Wherefore, as by one man sin entered into the world, and death by sin; and so death passed upon all men, for that all have sinned.

ROMANS 7:9

For I was alive without the law once: but when the commandment came, sin revived, and I died.

JOHN 3:3-5

Jesus answered and said unto him, Verily, verily, I say unto thee, Except a man be born again, he cannot see the kingdom of God. [4] Nicodemus saith unto him, How can a man be born when he is old? can he enter the second time into his mother's womb, and be born? [5] Jesus answered, Verily, verily, I say unto thee, Except a man be born of water and of the Spirit, he cannot enter into the kingdom of God.

JOHN 5:24

Verily, verily, I say unto you, He that heareth my word, and believeth on him that sent me, hath everlasting life, and shall not come into condemnation; but is passed from death unto life.

ROMANS 3:23

For all have sinned, and come short of the glory of God.

HEBREWS 12:23

To the general assembly and church of the firstborn, which are written in heaven, and to God the Judge of all, and to the spirits of just men made perfect.

JOHN 10:10

The thief cometh not, but for to steal, and to kill, and to destroy: I am come that they might have life, and that they might have it more abundantly.

ROMANS 6:16

Know ye not, that to whom ye yield yourselves servants to obey, his servants ye are to whom ye obey; whether of sin unto death, or of obedience unto righteousness?

INTRODUCTION
——PART II——
LOVING GOD

Now that you're born again, what's next?

God wants to establish some new patterns in your life. By taking the following "first steps" with Him, you'll lay a solid foundation for a growing relationship.

God's love for you won't change whether you do these things or not, but your love for Him will definitely be affected! You've been given the gift of a brand-new life, full of untold potential that's just waiting to be developed. Why settle for anything less than your divine destiny?

Fall deeply in love with God—He's worth it!

BE
BAPTIZED

Every born-again believer should be baptized in water. This isn't in order to be saved but rather because they've been saved.

> *Know ye not, that so many of us as were baptized into Jesus Christ were baptized into his death? Therefore we are buried with him by baptism into death: that like as Christ was raised up from the dead by the glory of the Father, even so we also should walk in newness of life.*
>
> ROMANS 6:3-4

Water baptism is an act of obedience to God's Word, symbolizing your baptism into the body of Christ.

You were immediately placed into the universal church upon your salvation. As a believer in Christ Jesus, you became part of His eternal body. **"There is one body, and one Spirit, even as ye are called in one hope of your calling; One Lord, one faith, one baptism, One God and Father of all, who is above all, and through all, and in you all"** (Eph. 4:4-6). You became a part of every believer who has ever believed on the Lord Jesus Christ. It doesn't matter if they go to your local church or if they believe exactly the same as you or not. You've been united with all the other believers in the body of Christ!

God's Word commands you to be baptized in water.

> *And he said unto them, Go ye into all the world, and preach the gospel to every creature. He that believeth and is baptized shall be saved; but he that believeth not shall be damned.*
>
> MARK 16:15-16

> *Go ye therefore, and teach all nations, baptizing them in the name of the Father, and of the Son, and of the Holy Ghost.*
>
> MATTHEW 28:19

Numerous examples from the book of Acts show how the early church spread the Gospel and obeyed this command. On the Day of Pentecost, those who were saved were water baptized (Acts 2:41). Philip water baptized the Ethiopian eunuch and the new converts in Samaria (Acts 8). Thus, the scriptural pattern given for us to follow today is baptism of new believers by immersion in water.

Being "baptized" as a child in a religious system where they sprinkled you with water is not sufficient. Also, you weren't scripturally baptized if it was done prior to your true conversion (i.e., as an infant or young child). The Bible makes it very clear that faith in Jesus is a prerequisite to water baptism (Acts 8:36-37). You must believe first and then be baptized.

A SIGN OF SALVATION

Although water baptism is an important first step in the Christian life, it's not required for salvation. Those who teach that water baptism is necessary to obtain your salvation are basing this on a misinterpretation of Acts 2:38, which says, **"Then Peter said unto them, Repent, and be baptized every one of you in the name of Jesus Christ for the remission of sins, and ye shall receive the gift of the Holy Ghost."** Some say this "proves" you must repent and be baptized for the remission of sins. The key to understanding this verse is the word **"for."** *For* often means "in order to obtain" but can also mean "as a result of," "because of," or "since." This verse says to repent, which means to put your faith in the Lord, and then to prove your faith in Him—as a result of being born again, because you've been born again, since you've been born again—by being water baptized. Those who believe that water baptism is required for salvation also teach that you must live in a system of religious works whereby you earn salvation by personal holiness. This is contrary to what the Word of God teaches.

Water baptism is a sign of salvation. In Acts 10, God told Cornelius, through an angel, to send for Peter in Joppa. When Peter came to Caesarea and began preaching to this man's entire household, they all received the baptism in the Holy Spirit, spoke in tongues, and prophesied. In light of this, Peter asked, **"Can any man forbid water, that these should not be baptized?"** (Acts 10:47). In other words, they were born again, had received the Holy Spirit, and then were baptized in water (Acts 10:44-48). Water baptism symbolized the salvation they had already received.

HOLY SPIRIT BAPTISM

Once you are born again and water baptized, your very next step should be to receive the power of the Holy Spirit. **"And when he had said this, he breathed on them, and saith unto them, Receive ye the Holy Ghost"** (John 20:22). God doesn't intend for you to live for Him on your own; He wants to live through you by the supernatural power of the Holy Spirit!

Jesus was baptized in the Holy Spirit.

> *Now when all the people were baptized, it came to pass, that Jesus also*
> *being baptized, and praying, the heaven was opened, And the Holy Ghost*
> *descended in a bodily shape like a dove upon him, and a voice came from*
> *heaven, which said, Thou art my beloved Son; in thee I am well pleased.*
> LUKE 3:21-22

> *The Spirit of the Lord is upon me, because he hath anointed me to preach*
> *the gospel to the poor; he hath sent me to heal the brokenhearted, to preach*
> *deliverance to the captives, and recovering of sight to the blind, to set at*
> *liberty them that are bruised, To preach the acceptable year of the Lord.*
> LUKE 4:18-19

If the Son of God Himself needed the Holy Spirit, how much more do we?

The gift of the Holy Spirit comes to all who ask in faith:

> *For every one that asketh receiveth; and he that seeketh findeth; and to him that knocketh it shall be opened. If a son shall ask bread of any of you that is a father, will he give him a stone? or if he ask a fish, will he for a fish give him a serpent? Or if he shall ask an egg, will he offer him a scorpion? If ye then, being evil, know how to give good gifts unto your children: how much more shall your heavenly Father give the Holy Spirit to them that ask him?*
>
> LUKE 11:10-13

Your heavenly Father knows how to give you good gifts. Ask Him in faith and you'll receive the baptism in the Holy Spirit too!

Both the Holy Spirit and water baptisms are clearly commanded in the Scriptures. The Lord will lead you into these two acts of faith and obedience as soon as you are born again. Both actions release tremendous benefits into your spiritual life!

For Further Information:

For more information, please refer to my in-depth look at the baptism in the Holy Spirit in the second half of this study guide.

—— OUTLINE ——

I. Every born-again believer should be baptized in water.

    A. This isn't in order to be saved but rather because they've been saved.

> *Know ye not, that so many of us as were baptized into Jesus Christ were baptized into his death? Therefore we are buried with him by baptism into death: that like as Christ was raised up from the dead by the glory of the Father, even so we also should walk in newness of life.*
>
> ROMANS 6:3-4

    B. Water baptism is an act of obedience to God's Word, symbolizing your baptism into the body of Christ.

    C. **"There is one body, and one Spirit, even as ye are called in one hope of your calling; One Lord, one faith, one baptism, One God and Father of all, who is above all, and through all, and in you all"** (Eph. 4:4-6).

    D. You became a part of every believer who has ever believed on the Lord Jesus Christ.

    E. God's Word commands you to be baptized in water.

> *And he said unto them, Go ye into all the world, and preach the gospel to every creature. He that believeth and is baptized shall be saved; but he that believeth not shall be damned.*
>
> MARK 16:15-16

> *Go ye therefore, and teach all nations, baptizing them in the name of the Father, and of the Son, and of the Holy Ghost.*
>
> MATTHEW 28:19

    F. Numerous examples from the book of Acts show how the early church spread the Gospel and obeyed this command.

    G. The Bible makes it very clear that faith in Jesus is a prerequisite to water baptism (Acts 8:36-37)—you must believe first and then be baptized.

II. Although water baptism is an important first step in the Christian life, it's not required for salvation.

    A. Those who teach that water baptism is necessary to obtain your salvation are basing this on a misinterpretation of Acts 2:38, which says, **"Then Peter said unto them, Repent, and be baptized every one of you in the name of Jesus Christ for the remission of sins, and ye shall receive the gift of the Holy Ghost."**

    B. Some say this "proves" you must repent and be baptized for the remission of sins.

C. The key to understanding this verse is the word **"for."** *For* often means "in order to obtain" but can also mean "as a result of," "because of," or "since."

D. This verse says to repent, which means to put your faith in the Lord, and then to prove your faith in Him—as a result of being born again, because you've been born again, since you've been born again—by being water baptized.

E. Those who believe that water baptism is required for salvation also teach that you must live in a system of religious works whereby you earn salvation by personal holiness, and this is contrary to what the Word of God teaches.

F. Water baptism symbolized the salvation they had already received.

III. Once you are born again and water baptized, your very next step should be to receive the power of the Holy Spirit.

A. God doesn't intend for you to live for Him on your own; He wants to live through you by the supernatural power of the Holy Spirit!

B. Jesus was baptized in the Holy Spirit.

> *Now when all the people were baptized, it came to pass, that Jesus also being baptized, and praying, the heaven was opened, And the Holy Ghost descended in a bodily shape like a dove upon him, and a voice came from heaven, which said, Thou art my beloved Son; in thee I am well pleased.*
> LUKE 3:21-22

> *The Spirit of the Lord is upon me, because he hath anointed me to preach the gospel to the poor; he hath sent me to heal the brokenhearted, to preach deliverance to the captives, and recovering of sight to the blind, to set at liberty them that are bruised, To preach the acceptable year of the Lord.*
> LUKE 4:18-19

C. If the Son of God Himself needed the Holy Spirit, how much more do you?

D. The gift of the Holy Spirit comes to all who ask in faith:

> *For every one that asketh receiveth; and he that seeketh findeth; and to him that knocketh it shall be opened. If a son shall ask bread of any of you that is a father, will he give him a stone? or if he ask a fish, will he for a fish give him a serpent? Or if he shall ask an egg, will he offer him a scorpion? If ye then, being evil, know how to give good gifts unto your children: how much more shall your heavenly Father give the Holy Spirit to them that ask him?*
> LUKE 11:10-13

E. Both the Holy Spirit and water baptisms are clearly commanded in the Scriptures.

F. The Lord will lead you into these two acts of faith and obedience as soon as you are born again.

G. Both actions release tremendous benefits into your spiritual life!

TEACHER'S
GUIDE

1. Every born-again believer should be baptized in water. This isn't in order to be saved but rather because they've been saved.

> *Know ye not, that so many of us as were baptized into Jesus Christ were baptized into his death? Therefore we are buried with him by baptism into death: that like as Christ was raised up from the dead by the glory of the Father, even so we also should walk in newness of life.*
>
> ROMANS 6:3-4

Water baptism is an act of obedience to God's Word, symbolizing your baptism into the body of Christ. **"There is one body, and one Spirit, even as ye are called in one hope of your calling; One Lord, one faith, one baptism, One God and Father of all, who is above all, and through all, and in you all"** (Eph. 4:4-6). You became a part of every believer who has ever believed on the Lord Jesus Christ. God's Word commands you to be baptized in water.

> *And he said unto them, Go ye into all the world, and preach the gospel to every creature. He that believeth and is baptized shall be saved; but he that believeth not shall be damned.*
>
> MARK 16:15-16

> *Go ye therefore, and teach all nations, baptizing them in the name of the Father, and of the Son, and of the Holy Ghost.*
>
> MATTHEW 28:19

Numerous examples from the book of Acts show how the early church spread the Gospel and obeyed this command. The Bible makes it very clear that faith in Jesus is a prerequisite to water baptism (Acts 8:36-37)—you must believe first and then be baptized.

    1a. Every born-again Christian should be baptized…
        A. In water
        B. In soy sauce
        C. Into the church
        D. All of the above
        E. None of the above
        A. In water
    1b. Are you baptized in order to be saved?
        No, you're baptized because you're saved
    1c. What are two passages of Scripture that command you to be baptized in water?
        Mark 16:15-16 and Matthew 28:19
    1d. True or false: Faith in Jesus is a prerequisite to water baptism.
        True

2. Although water baptism is an important first step in the Christian life, it's not required for salvation. Those who teach that water baptism is necessary to obtain your salvation are basing this on a misinterpretation of Acts 2:38, which says, **"Then Peter said unto them, Repent, and be baptized every one of you in the name of Jesus Christ for the remission of sins, and ye shall receive the gift of the Holy Ghost."** Some say this "proves" you must repent and be baptized for the remission of sins. The key to understanding this verse is the word **"for."** *For* often means "in order to obtain" but can also mean "as a result of," "because of," or "since." This verse says to repent, which means to put your faith in the Lord, and then to prove your faith in Him—as a result of being born again, because you've been born again, since you've been born again—by being water baptized. Those who believe that water baptism is required for salvation also teach that you must live in a system of religious works whereby you earn salvation by personal holiness, and this is contrary to what the Word of God teaches. Water baptism symbolized the salvation they had already received.

 2a. Is water baptism required for salvation?
  No
 2b. The teaching that water baptism is necessary to obtain salvation is based on what?
  A misinterpretation of Acts 2:38

3. Once you are born again and water baptized, your very next step should be to receive the power of the Holy Spirit. God doesn't intend for you to live for Him on your own; He wants to live through you by the supernatural power of the Holy Spirit! Jesus was baptized in the Holy Spirit.

> *Now when all the people were baptized, it came to pass, that Jesus also being baptized, and praying, the heaven was opened, And the Holy Ghost descended in a bodily shape like a dove upon him, and a voice came from heaven, which said, Thou art my beloved Son; in thee I am well pleased.*
> LUKE 3:21-22

> *The Spirit of the Lord is upon me, because he hath anointed me to preach the gospel to the poor; he hath sent me to heal the brokenhearted, to preach deliverance to the captives, and recovering of sight to the blind, to set at liberty them that are bruised, To preach the acceptable year of the Lord.*
> LUKE 4:18-19

If the Son of God Himself needed the Holy Spirit, how much more do you? The gift of the Holy Spirit comes to all who ask in faith:

> *For every one that asketh receiveth; and he that seeketh findeth; and to him that knocketh it shall be opened. If a son shall ask bread of any of you that is a father, will he give him a stone? or if he ask a fish, will he for a fish give him a serpent? Or if he shall ask an egg, will he offer him a scorpion? If ye then, being evil, know how to give good gifts unto your children: how much more shall your heavenly Father give the Holy Spirit to them that ask him?*
> LUKE 11:10-13

Both the Holy Spirit and water baptisms are clearly commanded in the Scriptures. The Lord will lead you into these two acts of faith and obedience as soon as you are born again. Both actions release tremendous benefits into your spiritual life!

3a. What is the next step after being born again and baptized in water?
   Receiving the power (baptism) of the Holy Spirit
3b. True or false: God intended for you to live for Him completely on your own.
   False
3c. The Lord will lead you into these two acts of _____ and _____ as soon as you are born again.
   Faith / obedience
3d. What will these actions do for you?
   They will release tremendous benefits in your life

DISCIPLESHIP
— QUESTIONS —

1. Every born-again Christian should be baptized...
    A. In water
    B. In soy sauce
    C. Into the church
    D. All of the above
    E. None of the above

2. Are you baptized in order to be saved?

    _____
    _____
    _____

3. What are two passages of Scripture that command you to be baptized in water?

    _____
    _____
    _____

4. True or false: Faith in Jesus is a prerequisite to water baptism.

5. Is water baptism required for salvation?

    _____
    _____
    _____

6. The teaching that water baptism is necessary to obtain salvation is based on what?

    _____
    _____
    _____

7. What is the next step after being born again and baptized in water?

    _____
    _____
    _____

8. True or false: God intended for you to live for Him completely on your own.

9. The Lord will lead you into these two acts of _____ and _____ as soon as you are born again.

10. What will these actions do for you?

_____

_____

_____

_____

ANSWER
—KEY—

1. A. In water

2. No, you're baptized because you're saved

3. Mark 16:15-16 and Matthew 28:19

4. True

5. No

6. A misinterpretation of Acts 2:38

7. Receiving the power (baptism) of the Holy Spirit

8. False

9. Faith / obedience

10. They will release tremendous benefits in your life

SCRIPTURES

ROMANS 6:3-4

Know ye not, that so many of us as were baptized into Jesus Christ were baptized into his death? [4] Therefore we are buried with him by baptism into death: that like as Christ was raised up from the dead by the glory of the Father, even so we also should walk in newness of life.

EPHESIANS 4:4-6

There is one body, and one Spirit, even as ye are called in one hope of your calling; [5] One Lord, one faith, one baptism, [6] One God and Father of all, who is above all, and through all, and in you all.

MARK 16:15-16

And he said unto them, Go ye into all the world, and preach the gospel to every creature. [16] He that believeth and is baptized shall be saved; but he that believeth not shall be damned.

MATTHEW 28:19

Go ye therefore, and teach all nations, baptizing them in the name of the Father, and of the Son, and of the Holy Ghost.

ACTS 2:41

Then they that gladly received his word were baptized: and the same day there were added unto them about three thousand souls.

ACTS 8:36-37

And as they went on their way, they came unto a certain water: and the eunuch said, See, here is water; what doth hinder me to be baptized? [37] And Philip said, If thou believest with all thine heart, thou mayest. And he answered and said, I believe that Jesus Christ is the Son of God.

ACTS 2:38

Then Peter said unto them, Repent, and be baptized every one of you in the name of Jesus Christ for the remission of sins, and ye shall receive the gift of the Holy Ghost.

ACTS 10:44-48

While Peter yet spake these words, the Holy Ghost fell on all them which heard the word. [45] And they of the circumcision which believed were astonished, as many as came with Peter, because that on the Gentiles also was poured out the gift of the Holy Ghost. [46] For they heard them speak with tongues, and magnify God. Then answered Peter, [47] Can any man forbid water, that these should not be baptized, which have received the Holy Ghost as well as we? [48] And he commanded them to be baptized in the name of the Lord. Then prayed they him to tarry certain days.

JOHN 20:22

And when he had said this, he breathed on them, and saith unto them, Receive ye the Holy Ghost.

LUKE 3:21-22

Now when all the people were baptized, it came to pass, that Jesus also being baptized, and praying, the heaven was opened, [22] And the Holy Ghost descended in a bodily shape like a dove upon him, and a voice came from heaven, which said, Thou art my beloved Son; in thee I am well pleased.

LUKE 4:18-19

The Spirit of the Lord is upon me, because he hath anointed me to preach the gospel to the poor; he hath sent me to heal the brokenhearted, to preach deliverance to the captives, and recovering of sight to the blind, to set at liberty them that are bruised, [19] To preach the acceptable year of the Lord.

LUKE 11:10-13

For every one that asketh receiveth; and he that seeketh findeth; and to him that knocketh it shall be opened. [11] If a son shall ask bread of any of you that is a father, will he give him a stone? or if he ask a fish, will he for a fish give him a serpent? [12] Or if he shall ask an egg, will he offer him a scorpion? [13] If ye then, being evil, know how to give good gifts unto your children: how much more shall your heavenly Father give the Holy Spirit to them that ask him?

BUILD
A SURE
FOUNDATION

The Bible is God's Word. He'll give you wisdom and guidance through it. **"As newborn babes, desire the sincere milk of the word, that ye may grow thereby"** (1 Pet. 2:2). As a baby draws sustenance from its mother's breast, so a new believer is nourished by spiritual milk from the Bible. You'll grow as you feed often on God's Word!

God's Word is God-breathed. **"All scripture is given by inspiration of God"** (2 Tim. 3:16). The Bible is charged with the very life of God, and it'll come alive to you as you read it. Through His Word, you'll get to know this awesome, loving God who has saved you. You'll grow in the grace and knowledge of Jesus Christ and become **"throughly furnished unto all good works"** (2 Tim. 3:17).

God will speak directly to you through the Bible.

> *For the word of God is quick, and powerful, and sharper than any twoedged sword, piercing even to the dividing asunder of soul and spirit, and of the joints and marrow, and is a discerner of the thoughts and intents of the heart.*
> HEBREWS 4:12

Don't just use your head to read this book; come to the Word with an open heart ready to receive from God!

Choose a version of the Bible that's easy to understand. God doesn't want language style to hinder you from getting to know Him. Personally, I use the *King James Version* because it's what I grew up on. However, you may find the old English phrases too difficult to understand. If that's the case, select a Bible to your liking, and read, study, and meditate on what it says. Any version you use is superior to not reading the Bible at all. The Holy Spirit can lead you to other translations later on, but laying a solid foundation of God's Word in your heart is what's most important right now.

GOD'S WORD—THE HIGHEST AUTHORITY

A basic understanding of the Bible is very helpful. I never went to seminary or Bible school, but I studied the Bible sixteen hours a day. It revolutionized my life! Some things I learned right away; others took me many years. But you can never exhaust the depths of God's Word. Everything you need for life and godliness can be found in it.

I wish somebody had explained to me the difference between the Old Covenant (Genesis through Malachi) and the New Covenant (Matthew through Revelation) when I was first saved. It took me a long time to discover that God deals with people totally differently from one covenant to the other. Most Christians see the Bible as one unit, all saying the same thing. They can't comprehend why the same God shows so much wrath and judgment in the Old Testament and so much grace and mercy in the New. They don't realize how everything changed between God and man once Jesus Christ came to earth. You and I are in the New Covenant in Christ Jesus!

Guidance from mature believers can save you time and painful mistakes, but always check it against God's Word for yourself. Be careful only to receive what's right, because people can steer you in the wrong direction. That's why comparing everything they say with the Bible to see how it matches up is so important. Let go of what doesn't line up, and hold on to what does. God's Word must be the highest authority in your life.

The Word of God is powerful! It's not just a book written by man about God. Some people raise questions about the Bible and say there are many inconsistencies within it. Many good books (called "apologetics") answer these questions and validate the authority of the Bible. The Word is actually a book by God speaking to you through man. All the books in the Bible are supernaturally inspired and have been protected and preserved error free. Your job is to interpret and believe God's Word as it was written. If you do, God Himself will fellowship with you—and that's awesome!

For Further Information:

My teaching *A Sure Foundation* will help you understand how important God's Word is to your life.

— OUTLINE —

I. The Bible is God's Word—He'll give you wisdom and guidance through it.

   A. **"As newborn babes, desire the sincere milk of the word, that ye may grow thereby"** (1 Pet. 2:2).

   B. You'll grow as you feed often on God's Word!

   C. God's Word is God-breathed: **"All scripture is given by inspiration of God"** (2 Tim. 3:16).

   D. Through His Word, you'll get to know this awesome, loving God who has saved you.

   E. You'll grow in the grace and knowledge of Jesus Christ and become **"throughly furnished unto all good works"** (2 Tim. 3:17).

   F. God will speak directly to you through the Bible.

   > *For the word of God is quick, and powerful, and sharper than any twoedged sword, piercing even to the dividing asunder of soul and spirit, and of the joints and marrow, and is a discerner of the thoughts and intents of the heart.*
   > HEBREWS 4:12

   G. Don't just use your head to read this book; come to the Word with an open heart ready to receive from God!

   H. Choose a version of the Bible that's easy to understand—God doesn't want language style to hinder you from getting to know Him.

   I. Any version you use is superior to not reading the Bible at all.

   J. The Holy Spirit can lead you to other translations later on, but laying a solid foundation of God's Word in your heart is what's most important right now.

II. A basic understanding of the Bible is very helpful.

   A. But you can never exhaust the depths of God's Word.

   B. Everything you need for life and godliness can be found in it.

   C. Most Christians see the Bible as one unit, all saying the same thing.

   D. They don't realize how everything changed between God and man once Jesus Christ came to earth.

   E. You and I are in the New Covenant in Christ Jesus!

F. Guidance from mature believers can save you time and painful mistakes, but always check it against God's Word for yourself.

G. Let go of what doesn't line up, and hold on to what does.

H. God's Word must be the highest authority in your life.

I. The Word is actually a book by God speaking to you through man.

J. All the books in the Bible are supernaturally inspired and have been protected and preserved error free.

K. Your job is to interpret and believe God's Word as it was written.

L. If you do, God Himself will fellowship with you—and that's awesome!

TEACHER'S GUIDE

1. The Bible is God's Word—He'll give you wisdom and guidance through it. **"As newborn babes, desire the sincere milk of the word, that ye may grow thereby"** (1 Pet. 2:2). You'll grow as you feed often on God's Word! God's Word is God-breathed: **"All scripture is given by inspiration of God"** (2 Tim. 3:16). Through His Word, you'll get to know this awesome, loving God who has saved you. You'll grow in the grace and knowledge of Jesus Christ and become **"throughly furnished unto all good works"** (2 Tim. 3:17). God will speak directly to you through the Bible.

> *For the word of God is quick, and powerful, and sharper than any twoedged*
> *sword, piercing even to the dividing asunder of soul and spirit, and of the*
> *joints and marrow, and is a discerner of the thoughts and intents of the heart.*
> HEBREWS 4:12

Don't just use your head to read this book; come to the Word with an open heart ready to receive from God! Choose a version of the Bible that's easy to understand—God doesn't want language style to hinder you from getting to know Him. Any version you use is superior to not reading the Bible at all. The Holy Spirit can lead you to other translations later on, but laying a solid foundation of God's Word in your heart is what's most important right now.

1a. How does God give you wisdom and guidance?
Through the Bible, His Word
1b. First Peter 2:2 says, **"As newborn babes, _____ the sincere milk of the word, that ye may grow thereby."**
"Desire"
1c. True or false: God's Word is God-breathed.
True
1d. How are you to approach the Word when you read it?
Not with your head—but with an open heart ready to receive
1e. Any version you use is _____ to _____ reading the Bible at all.
Superior / not

2. A basic understanding of the Bible is very helpful. But you can never exhaust the depths of God's Word. Everything you need for life and godliness can be found in it. Most Christians see the Bible as one unit, all saying the same thing. They don't realize how everything changed between God and man once Jesus Christ came to earth. You and I are in the New Covenant in Christ Jesus! Guidance from mature believers can save you time and painful mistakes, but always check it against God's Word for yourself. Let go of what doesn't line up, and hold on to what does. God's Word must be the highest authority in your life. The Word is actually a book by God speaking to you through man. All the books in the Bible are supernaturally inspired and have been protected and preserved error free. Your job is to interpret and believe God's Word as it was written. If you do, God Himself will fellowship with you—and that's awesome!

2a. True or false: You can exhaust the depths of God's Word.
   False

2b. Most Christians see the Bible as one unit, all saying the same thing—what is it that they don't realize?
   How everything changed between God and man once Jesus Christ came to earth

2c. Guidance from mature believers can save you time and painful mistakes, but what should you always do?
   Check it against God's Word for yourself

2d. Must God's Word be the highest authority in your life?
   Yes

2e. What is the Word?
   A. A good paperweight
   B. A book written by man about God
   C. A book by God speaking to you through man
   D. All of the above
   E. None of the above
   C. A book by God speaking to you through man

2f. What is your job now?
   To interpret and believe God's Word as it was written

DISCIPLESHIP
—— QUESTIONS ——

1. How does God give you wisdom and guidance?

   _____

   _____

   _____

2. First Peter 2:2 says, **"As newborn babes, _____ the sincere milk of the word, that ye may grow thereby."**

3. True or false: God's Word is God-breathed.

4. How are you to approach the Word when you read it?

   _____

   _____

   _____

5. Any version you use is _____ to _____ reading the Bible at all.

6. True or false: You can exhaust the depths of God's Word.

7. Most Christians see the Bible as one unit, all saying the same thing—what is it that they don't realize?

   _____

   _____

   _____

8. Guidance from mature believers can save you time and painful mistakes, but what should you always do?

   _____

   _____

   _____

9. Must God's Word be the highest authority in your life?

   _____

   _____

   _____

10. What is the Word?
    A. A good paperweight
    B. A book written by man about God
    C. A book by God speaking to you through man
    D. All of the above
    E. None of the above

11. What is your job now?

    _____
    _____
    _____

ANSWER
—KEY—

1. Through the Bible, His Word

2. **"Desire"**

3. True

4. Not with your head—but with an open heart ready to receive

5. Superior / not

6. False

7. How everything changed between God and man once Jesus Christ came to earth

8. Check it against God's Word for yourself

9. Yes

10. C. A book by God speaking to you through man

11. To interpret and believe God's Word as it was written

—— SCRIPTURES ——

1 PETER 2:2

As newborn babes, desire the sincere milk of the word, that ye may grow thereby.

2 TIMOTHY 3:16-17

All scripture is given by inspiration of God, and is profitable for doctrine, for reproof, for correction, for instruction in righteousness: [17] That the man of God may be perfect, throughly furnished unto all good works.

HEBREWS 4:12

For the word of God is quick, and powerful, and sharper than any twoedged sword, piercing even to the dividing asunder of soul and spirit, and of the joints and marrow, and is a discerner of the thoughts and intents of the heart.

JOIN A LOCAL CHURCH

Every step I've mentioned so far—being water baptized, receiving the baptism in the Holy Spirit, building a sure foundation in the Word of God—can be made much easier if you get involved in a good local church.

The Lord created the church, which is simply a group of His people who meet together regularly for the purpose of loving each other, praying for each other, and building each other up. It doesn't always function that way, but it's still the greatest institution on earth!

Many people love the Lord but don't like His people. That's because some Christians don't reflect God like they should. They hurt others with their mean-spiritedness and hypocrisy. Jesus faced the same thing—unbelievers welcomed Him, while religious folks persecuted Him. Because of this, you may want to commit your life to Christ and enjoy a relationship with Him but have nothing to do with a church. I can relate to what you're feeling, but that's a wrong attitude to keep. It's like fixing a leaky boat—better to be inside making repairs than outside in the ocean where you could drown!

COALS STAY HOT IN THE FIRE

You grow spiritually by participating in a good church. As a believer, you're like a hot coal in a burning fire. You'll stay red hot and glowing as long as you're involved with other believers in a local church body. Separate and isolate yourself from the other coals, and it won't be long before you grow cold. Stay in the fire! Although there are plenty of bad churches out there, it's worth your effort to find the good ones. Every believer needs to be involved in a local church.

You can learn a lot from Christians who have walked in God's Word and have been through some things. It's important not to believe just anyone; God will place spiritual leaders in your life for the purpose of helping you grow.

> *And he gave some, apostles; and some, prophets; and some, evangelists; and some, pastors and teachers; For the perfecting of the saints, for the work of the ministry, for the edifying of the body of Christ.*
> EPHESIANS 4:11-12

Many new believers want to bypass people and receive everything they need straight from God. However, the Lord prefers to work through mature Christians to build up and strengthen newer ones.

God uses apostles, prophets, evangelists, pastors, and teachers to equip and mature believers for the work of the ministry. He gave these people to build up the body of Christ until **"we all come in the unity of the faith, and of the knowledge of the Son of God, unto a perfect man, unto the measure of the stature of the fulness of Christ"** (Eph. 4:13). Since the church hasn't fully attained that yet, God is still using these five different types of ministry gifts to accomplish His goals. It's important that you submit to the Lord's system.

You are disobeying God if you don't get involved with other believers. God will still love you and you won't lose your salvation, but you'll be a cold, isolated coal when you run into hurts and difficult situations. Instead of having a strong support system of other believers who love you and know your situation, you'll be on your own in the ocean. You definitely need to participate in a good church!

RELATIONSHIP WITH HIS PEOPLE

What you hear while you're young in the Lord will greatly impact your spiritual development. As a new believer, you're like a little plant that needs to be in a protected environment until your roots grow deep. When I was young in my faith, I'd walk out in the middle of a service if I heard something contrary to God's Word being preached. Today I don't just get up and leave, because I know it won't hurt me the way it would've when I was first born again. However, I don't subject myself to wrong teaching again and again, because it's unwise. If you hear something enough, you'll start to believe it. Since you are forming your spiritual root structures, it's crucial that you hear correct teaching now.

Although what you hear as a new believer is important, a church will supply you with more than just teaching. Your participation in a local body can provide you with needed fellowship and relationships with other Christians. Media ministries like mine can feed you God's Word through audio messages, books, websites, radio, and television programs, but nothing helps the Word become flesh in your life better than regular interaction with other on-fire believers.

Christianity is a relationship with God and His people. Before his conversion, Paul (then named Saul) hated Christians. While on his way to Damascus to kill more believers, the Lord appeared to him in a blinding flash of light (Acts 9:1-5). Jesus asked, "Why are you persecuting Me?" Notice that His question wasn't "Why are you persecuting My people?" That's because the Lord becomes one with every individual who puts his or her faith in Him. If someone touches you, they touch the apple of God's eye. God loves you the same as He loves every other Christian!

God demonstrates His love through His people.

> *By this shall all men know that ye are my disciples, if ye have love one to another.*
>
> JOHN 13:35

> *If a man say, I love God, and hateth his brother, he is a liar: for he that loveth not his brother whom he hath seen, how can he love God whom he hath not seen?*
>
> 1 JOHN 4:20

No one who refuses to relate to God's people can say they truly have a relationship with God.

PUT HIS WORD INTO PRACTICE

A local church will provide you with the opportunity to put Christ's teachings into practice. It's one thing to hear the Word say to do unto others as you would have them do unto you (Matt. 7:12), but it's quite another to actually live it. Your rate of maturity will slow down if all you ever do is shut yourself up with a Bible for weeks and months. Some things you'll never really learn until you have to deal with other people. From God's perspective, you don't really know something from His Word until you've put it into practice.

Your local church leadership can provide ministry to you and your loved ones in practical ways that a media/traveling ministry cannot. I can teach you God's Word concerning healing, but I won't be available when you need to **"call for the elders of the church"** (James 5:14) to come over to your house and anoint the sick. However, the leaders of your local church can do that and so much more. They can officiate weddings, perform funerals, minister to your children, advise you from the Word, pray about specific situations, and serve as godly role models you can personally interact with on a regular basis. Your entire household will benefit from your participation in a local church!

You'll also find like-minded believers with whom you can establish close friendships. The two most important influences in your life are what you hear/read and the person(s) you spend your time with. This doesn't mean you reject people who aren't believers, but from now on, your strongest friendships should be with other Christians (2 Cor. 6:14-18). If you remain unequally yoked with an unbeliever, sooner or later, that person will negatively affect you. **"He that walketh with wise men shall be wise: but a companion of fools shall be destroyed"** (Prov. 13:20). You always rise or sink to the level of your closest friends.

Regularly meeting together with other believers protects and promotes your spiritual health.

> *Let us hold fast the profession of our faith without wavering; (for he is faithful that promised;) And let us consider one another to provoke unto love and to good works: Not forsaking the assembling of ourselves together, as the manner of some is; but exhorting one another: and so much the more, as ye see the day approaching.*
>
> HEBREWS 10:23-25

Plug yourself into a good local church!

FIND A GOOD CHURCH

Don't let minor doctrinal issues prevent you from settling into a good church. If the differences are just some external matters and not core beliefs, I suggest you stay involved.

Even if it's not a strong faith-teaching church, it's better to participate in some local church than not to participate at all. There are other important benefits you can gain from participating. If you live in an area where you have a choice, always choose a church that preaches the whole counsel of God!

A good church preaches everything God offers in His Word—salvation, baptism in the Holy Spirit, the gifts of the Spirit, healing, deliverance, and prosperity. The denomination I grew up in centered all of the preaching on just the forgiveness of sins. Many people (like me) got saved, but they didn't believe that God's miraculous power was for today. When my father (a leader in that church) became seriously ill, my family and I didn't know how to receive healing from the Lord. No one in our church had faith for it, because we were never taught healing from God's Word. My father died at fifty-four years of age, leaving me fatherless at twelve and my mother a widow at thirty-eight. Much pain came into our lives as a result of this. Our church didn't cause this problem, but it sure didn't equip us to overcome it either.

Be part of a church that teaches the whole counsel of God. Don't stay somewhere that's against the baptism in the Holy Spirit, the gifts of the Holy Spirit, healing, and so on. Having your name on a pew or your aunt as the choir director won't help when you're sick. Although you're personally aware that God heals, you'll be frustrated when you have trouble receiving it, because you don't know God's Word. To receive prosperity, deliverance, or whatever, you need to be taught God's Word. Be part of a church you can wholeheartedly support!

A good church preaches faith and grace for the entire Christian life, not just forgiveness of your sins. Many groups teach that all you need to do to initially receive is believe but that after you're saved, everything is based on your performance. That's wrong! You don't have to earn God's favor, earn answers to prayer, earn God's love, earn your healing, or earn anything else. Everything God gives you is by grace through faith.

The atmosphere ought to encourage healthy relationships. The pastor should set the tone by being a loving person. It's not necessarily better to go to a big church or a small one. Some big churches have small groups for the purpose of nurturing and maturing believers. Often, small churches naturally have an environment conducive to building friendships and spiritual growth. Whether big or small, your experience in a church will normally come down to the quality of your relationships there.

Trust the Lord to lead you to a good local church. Pray. Then take some steps of faith. It's His good pleasure to guide you to your place in His body!

—— OUTLINE ——

I. Every step I've mentioned so far—being water baptized, receiving the baptism in the Holy Spirit, building a sure foundation in the Word of God—can be made much easier if you get involved in a good local church.

    A. The Lord created the church, which is simply a group of His people who meet together regularly for the purpose of loving each other, praying for each other, and building each other up.

    B. Many people love the Lord but don't like His people.

    C. That's because some Christians don't reflect God like they should.

    D. They hurt others with their mean-spiritedness and hypocrisy.

    E. Because of this, you may want to commit your life to Christ and enjoy a relationship with Him but have nothing to do with a church.

    F. I can relate to what you're feeling, but that's a wrong attitude to keep.

II. You grow spiritually by participating in a good church.

    A. As a believer, you're like a hot coal in a burning fire—you'll stay red hot and glowing as long as you're involved with other believers in a local church body.

    B. Separate and isolate yourself from the other coals, and it won't be long before you grow cold.

    C. Although there are plenty of bad churches out there, it's worth your effort to find the good ones—every believer needs to be involved in a local church.

    D. You can learn a lot from Christians who have walked in God's Word and have been through some things.

> *And he gave some, apostles; and some, prophets; and some, evangelists; and some, pastors and teachers; For the perfecting of the saints, for the work of the ministry, for the edifying of the body of Christ.*
> EPHESIANS 4:11-12

    E. Many new believers want to bypass people and receive everything they need straight from God.

    F. However, the Lord prefers to work through mature Christians to build up and strengthen newer ones.

    G. God uses apostles, prophets, evangelists, pastors, and teachers to equip and mature believers for the work of the ministry.

H. He gave these people to build up the body of Christ until **"we all come in the unityof the faith, and of the knowledge of the Son of God, unto a perfect man, unto the measure of the stature of the fulness of Christ"** (Eph. 4:13).

I. Since the church hasn't fully attained that yet, God is still using these five different types of ministry gifts to accomplish His goals.

J. You are disobeying God if you don't get involved with other believers.

K. God will still love you and you won't lose your salvation, but you'll be a cold, isolated coal when you run into hurts and difficult situations.

L. Instead of having a strong support system of other believers who love you and know your situation, you'll be on your own in the ocean.

III. What you hear while you're young in the Lord will greatly impact your spiritual development.

A. As a new believer, you're like a little plant that needs to be in a protected environment until your roots grow deep.

B. Since you are forming your spiritual root structures, it's crucial that you hear correct teaching now.

C. Although what you hear as a new believer is important, a church will supply you with more than just teaching.

D. Your participation in a local body can provide you with needed fellowship and relationships with other Christians.

E. Media ministries can feed you God's Word through audio messages, books, websites, radio, and television programs, but nothing helps the Word become flesh in your life better than regular interaction with other on-fire believers.

F. God demonstrates His love through His people.

> *By this shall all men know that ye are my disciples, if ye have love one to another.*
>
> JOHN 13:35

> *If a man say, I love God, and hateth his brother, he is a liar: for he that loveth not his brother whom he hath seen, how can he love God whom he hath not seen?*
>
> 1 JOHN 4:20

G. No one who refuses to relate to God's people can say they truly have a relationship with God.

IV. A local church will provide you with the opportunity to put Christ's teachings into practice.

A. It's one thing to hear the Word say to do unto others as you would have them do unto you (Matt. 7:12), but it's quite another to actually live it.

B. Your rate of maturity will slow down if all you ever do is shut yourself up with a Bible for weeks and months.

C. Some things you'll never really learn until you have to deal with other people.

D. Your local church leadership can provide ministry to you and your loved ones in practical ways that a media/traveling ministry cannot.

E. You'll also find like-minded believers with whom you can establish close friendships.

F. This doesn't mean you reject people who aren't believers, but from now on, your strongest friendships should be with other Christians (2 Cor. 6:14-18).

G. If you remain unequally yoked with an unbeliever, sooner or later, that person will negatively affect you—**"He that walketh with wise men shall be wise: but a companion of fools shall be destroyed"** (Prov. 13:20).

H. You always rise or sink to the level of your closest friends.

I. Regularly meeting together with other believers protects and promotes your spiritual health.

> *Let us hold fast the profession of our faith without wavering; (for he is faithful that promised;) And let us consider one another to provoke unto love and to good works: Not forsaking the assembling of ourselves together, as the manner of some is; but exhorting one another: and so much the more, as ye see the day approaching.*
>
> HEBREWS 10:23-25

V. Don't let minor doctrinal issues prevent you from settling into a good church.

A. Even if it's not a strong faith-teaching church, it's better to participate in some local church than not to participate at all.

B. A good church preaches everything God offers in His Word—salvation, baptism in the Holy Spirit, the gifts of the Spirit, healing, deliverance, and prosperity.

C. Don't stay somewhere that's against the baptism in the Holy Spirit, the gifts of the Holy Spirit, healing, and so on.

D. Many groups teach that all you need to do to initially receive is believe but that after you're saved, everything is based on your performance—that's wrong!

E. You don't have to earn God's favor, earn answers to prayer, earn God's love, earn your healing, or earn anything else.

F. The atmosphere ought to encourage healthy relationships.

G. Whether big or small, your experience in a church will normally come down to the quality of your relationships there.

H. Trust the Lord to lead you to a good local church.

I. Pray—then take some steps of faith.

J. It's His good pleasure to guide you to your place in His body!

TEACHER'S
GUIDE

1. Every step I've mentioned so far—being water baptized, receiving the baptism in the Holy Spirit, building a sure foundation in the Word of God—can be made much easier if you get involved in a good local church. The Lord created the church, which is simply a group of His people who meet together regularly for the purpose of loving each other, praying for each other, and building each other up. Many people love the Lord but don't like His people. That's because some Christians don't reflect God like they should. They hurt others with their mean-spiritedness and hypocrisy. Because of this, you may want to commit your life to Christ and enjoy a relationship with Him but have nothing to do with a church. I can relate to what you're feeling, but that's a wrong attitude to keep.

1a. How can steps in your Christian walk—such as being water baptized, receiving the baptism in the Holy Spirit, and building a sure foundation in the Word of God—be made easier?
   A. By joining a local church
   B. By wishing and hoping
   C. By paying someone
   D. All of the above
   E. None of the above
   A. By joining a local church

1b. According to the lesson, what is the church?
   A group of the Lord's people who meet together regularly for the purpose of loving each other, praying for each other, and building each other up

1c. True or false: Wanting to commit your life to Christ and enjoy a relationship with Him but having nothing to do with a church is a proper attitude to have.
   False

2. You grow spiritually by participating in a good church. As a believer, you're like a hot coal in a burning fire—you'll stay red hot and glowing as long as you're involved with other believers in a local church body. Separate and isolate yourself from the other coals, and it won't be long before you grow cold. Although there are plenty of bad churches out there, it's worth your effort to find the good ones—every believer needs to be involved in a local church. You can learn a lot from Christians who have walked in God's Word and have been through some things.

> *And he gave some, apostles; and some, prophets; and some, evangelists; and some, pastors and teachers; For the perfecting of the saints, for the work of the ministry, for the edifying of the body of Christ.*
>
> EPHESIANS 4:11-12

Many new believers want to bypass people and receive everything they need straight from God. However, the Lord prefers to work through mature Christians to build up and strengthen newer ones. God uses apostles, prophets, evangelists, pastors, and teachers to equip and mature believers for the work of the ministry. He gave these people to build up the body of Christ until **"we all come in the unity of the faith, and of the knowledge of the Son of God, unto a perfect man, unto the measure of the stature of the fulness of Christ"** (Eph. 4:13). Since the church hasn't fully attained that yet, God is still using these five different types of ministry gifts to accomplish His goals. You are disobeying God if you don't get involved with other believers. God will still love you and you won't lose your salvation, but you'll be a cold, isolated coal when you run into hurts and difficult situations. Instead of having a strong support system of other believers who love you and know your situation, you'll be on your own in the ocean.

2a. You _____ _____ by participating in a good church.
Grow spiritually

2b. Separate and isolate yourself from other coals—other believers in a local church body—and it won't be long before what?
A. You grow cold
B. You grow stronger
C. Nothing happens
D. All of the above
E. None of the above
A. You grow cold

2c. "And he gave some, apostles; and some, prophets; and some, evangelists; and some, pastors and teachers; For the _____ of the saints, for the work of the ministry, for the edifying of the body of Christ" (Eph. 4:11-12).
"Perfecting"

2d. Are you disobeying God if you don't get involved with other believers?
Yes

3. What you hear while you're young in the Lord will greatly impact your spiritual development. As a new believer, you're like a little plant that needs to be in a protected environment until your roots grow deep. Since you are forming your spiritual root structures, it's crucial that you hear correct teaching now. Although what you hear as a new believer is important, a church will supply you with more than just teaching. Your participation in a local body can provide you with needed fellowship and relationships with other Christians. Media ministries can feed you God's Word through audio messages, books, websites, radio, and television programs, but nothing helps the Word become flesh in your life better than regular interaction with other on-fire believers. God demonstrates His love through His people.

> *By this shall all men know that ye are my disciples, if ye have love one to another.*
>
> JOHN 13:35

> *If a man say, I love God, and hateth his brother, he is a liar: for he that loveth not his brother whom he hath seen, how can he love God whom he hath not seen?*
>
> 1 JOHN 4:20

No one who refuses to relate to God's people can say they truly have a relationship with God.

3a. What you hear while you're young in the Lord will greatly impact your spiritual development—why?
Because as a new believer, you're like a little plant that needs to be in a protected environment until your roots grow deep, and since you are forming spiritual root structures, it's crucial that you hear correct teaching now

3b. God demonstrates His _____ through His people—**"By this shall all men know that ye are my disciples, if ye have _____ one to another"** (John 13:35).
Love / "love"

3c. True or false: Those who refuse to relate to God's people can say they truly have a relationship with God.
False

4. A local church will provide you with the opportunity to put Christ's teachings into practice. It's one thing to hear the Word say to do unto others as you would have them do unto you (Matt. 7:12), but it's quite another to actually live it. Your rate of maturity will slow down if all you ever do is shut yourself up with a Bible for weeks and months. Some things you'll never really learn until you have to deal with other people. Your local church leadership can provide ministry to you and your loved ones in practical ways that a media/traveling ministry cannot. You'll also find like-minded believers with whom you can establish close friendships. This doesn't mean you reject people who aren't believers, but from now on, your strongest friendships should be with other Christians (2 Cor. 6:14-18). If you remain unequally yoked with an unbeliever, sooner or later, that person will negatively affect you—**"He that walketh with wise men shall be wise: but a companion of fools shall be destroyed"** (Prov. 13:20). You always rise or sink to the level of your closest friends. Regularly meeting together with other believers protects and promotes your spiritual health.

> *Let us hold fast the profession of our faith without wavering; (for he is faithful that promised;) And let us consider one another to provoke unto love and to good works: Not forsaking the assembling of ourselves together, as the manner of some is; but exhorting one another: and so much the more, as ye see the day approaching.*
>
> HEBREWS 10:23-25

4a. If all you ever do is shut yourself up with a Bible for weeks and months, what will happen to your rate of maturity?
    A. It will slow down
    B. It will speed up
    C. It will stay the same
    D. All of the above
    E. None of the above
    A. It will slow down

4b. Once you are born again, whom should your strongest friendships be with and why?
    With other Christians (2 Cor. 6:14-18), because if you remain unequally yoked with an unbeliever, sooner or later, that person will negatively affect you (Prov. 13:20)

4c. You always _____ or _____ to the level of your closest friends.
    Rise / sink

JOIN A LOCAL CHURCH

5. Don't let minor doctrinal issues prevent you from settling into a good church. Even if it's not a strong faith-teaching church, it's better to participate in some local church than not to participate at all. A good church preaches everything God offers in His Word—salvation, baptism in the Holy Spirit, the gifts of the Spirit, healing, deliverance, and prosperity. Don't stay somewhere that's against the baptism in the Holy Spirit, the gifts of the Holy Spirit, healing, and so on. Many groups teach that all you need to do to initially receive is believe but that after you're saved, everything is based on your performance—that's wrong! You don't have to earn God's favor, earn answers to prayer, earn God's love, earn your healing, or earn anything else. The atmosphere ought to encourage healthy relationships. Whether big or small, your experience in a church will normally come down to the quality of your relationships there. Trust the Lord to lead you to a good local church. Pray—then take some steps of faith. It's His good pleasure to guide you to your place in His body!

5a. True or false: You shouldn't let minor doctrinal issues prevent you from settling into a good church.
True

5b. Is it better or worse to participate in a local church, even if it's not a strong faith-teaching one, than not to participate at all?
Better

5c. Should you stay at a church that doesn't preach everything God offers in His Word?
No

5d. What should the atmosphere of your church do?
Encourage healthy relationships

DISCIPLESHIP
—— QUESTIONS ——

1. How can steps in your Christian walk—such as being water baptized, receiving the baptism in the Holy Spirit, and building a sure foundation in the Word of God—be made easier?
    A. By joining a local church
    B. By wishing and hoping
    C. By paying someone
    D. All of the above
    E. None of the above

2. According to the lesson, what is the church?

    _____

    _____

    _____

3. True or false: Wanting to commit your life to Christ and enjoy a relationship with Him but having nothing to do with a church is a proper attitude to have.

4. You _____ _____ by participating in a good church.

5. Separate and isolate yourself from other coals—other believers in a local church body—and it won't be long before what?
    A. You grow cold
    B. You grow stronger
    C. Nothing happens
    D. All of the above
    E. None of the above

6. **"And he gave some, apostles; and some, prophets; and some, evangelists; and some, pastors and teachers; For the _____ of the saints, for the work of the ministry, for the edifying of the body of Christ"** (Eph. 4:11-12).

7. Are you disobeying God if you don't get involved with other believers?

    _____

    _____

    _____

8. What you hear while you're young in the Lord will greatly impact your spiritual development—why?

_____

_____

_____

9. God demonstrates His _____ through His people—**"By this shall all men know that ye are my disciples, if ye have _____ one to another"** (John 13:35).

10. True or false: Those who refuse to relate to God's people can say they truly have a relationship with God.

11. If all you ever do is shut yourself up with a Bible for weeks and months, what will happen to your rate of maturity?
    A. It will slow down
    B. It will speed up
    C. It will stay the same
    D. All of the above
    E. None of the above

12. Once you are born again, whom should your strongest friendships be with and why?

_____

_____

_____

13. You always _____ or _____ to the level of your closest friends.

14. True or false: You shouldn't let minor doctrinal issues prevent you from settling into a good church.

15. Is it better or worse to participate in a local church, even if it's not a strong faith-teaching one, than not to participate at all?

_____

_____

_____

16. Should you stay at a church that doesn't preach everything God offers in His Word?

_____

_____

_____

17. What should the atmosphere of your church do?

_____

_____

_____

_____

ANSWER
—KEY—

1. A. By joining a local church

2. A group of the Lord's people who meet together regularly for the purpose of loving each other, praying for each other, and building each other up

3. False

4. Grow spiritually

5. A. You grow cold

6. **"Perfecting"**

7. Yes

8. Because as a new believer, you're like a little plant that needs to be in a protected environment until your roots grow deep, and since you are forming spiritual root structures, it's crucial that you hear correct teaching now

9. Love / **"love"**

10. False

11. A. It will slow down

12. With other Christians (2 Cor. 6:14-18), because if you remain unequally yoked with an unbeliever, sooner or later, that person will negatively affect you (Prov. 13:20)

13. Rise / sink

14. True

15. Better

16. No

17. Encourage healthy relationships

—— SCRIPTURES ——

EPHESIANS 4:11-13

And he gave some, apostles; and some, prophets; and some, evangelists; and some, pastors and teachers; [12] For the perfecting of the saints, for the work of the ministry, for the edifying of the body of Christ: [13] Till we all come in the unity of the faith, and of the knowledge of the Son of God, unto a perfect man, unto the measure of the stature of the fulness of Christ.

ACTS 9:1-5

And Saul, yet breathing out threatenings and slaughter against the disciples of the Lord, went unto the high priest, [2] And desired of him letters to Damascus to the synagogues, that if he found any of this way, whether they were men or women, he might bring them bound unto Jerusalem. [3] And as he journeyed, he came near Damascus: and suddenly there shined round about him a light from heaven: [4] And he fell to the earth, and heard a voice saying unto him, Saul, Saul, why persecutest thou me? [5] And he said, Who art thou, Lord? And the Lord said, I am Jesus whom thou persecutest: it is hard for thee to kick against the pricks.

JOHN 13:35

By this shall all men know that ye are my disciples, if ye have love one to another.

1 JOHN 4:20

If a man say, I love God, and hateth his brother, he is a liar: for he that loveth not his brother whom he hath seen, how can he love God whom he hath not seen?

MATTHEW 7:12

Therefore all things whatsoever ye would that men should do to you, do ye even so to them: for this is the law and the prophets.

JAMES 5:14

Is any sick among you? let him call for the elders of the church; and let them pray over him, anointing him with oil in the name of the Lord.

2 CORINTHIANS 6:14-18

Be ye not unequally yoked together with unbelievers: for what fellowship hath righteousness with unrighteousness? and what communion hath light with darkness? [15] And what concord hath Christ with Belial? or what part hath he that believeth with an infidel? [16] And what agreement hath the temple of God with idols? for ye are the temple of the living God; as God hath said, I will dwell in them, and walk in them; and I will be their God, and they shall be my people. [17] Wherefore come out from among them, and be ye separate, saith the Lord, and touch not the unclean thing; and I will receive you, [18] And will be a Father unto you, and ye shall be my sons and daughters, saith the Lord Almighty.

PROVERBS 13:20

He that walketh with wise men shall be wise: but a companion of fools shall be destroyed.

HEBREWS 10:23-25

Let us hold fast the profession of our faith without wavering; (for he is faithful that promised;) [24] And let us consider one another to provoke unto love and to good works: [25] Not forsaking the assembling of ourselves together, as the manner of some is; but exhorting one another: and so much the more, as ye see the day approaching.

KNOW
HIM
INTIMATELY

God saved you for the purpose of enjoying an intimate relationship with Him from now on. Salvation isn't just "insurance" from hell's flames. Neither does God intend that you receive forgiveness for your sins and then merely survive until heaven. Salvation is so much more!

For God so loved the world, that he gave his only begotten Son, that
whosoever believeth in him should not perish, but have everlasting life.
JOHN 3:16

And this is life eternal, that they might know thee the only true God, and
Jesus Christ, whom thou hast sent.
JOHN 17:3

Salvation is getting to know this awesome, wonderful, loving God for the rest of eternity!

Jesus came to give you eternal life. The idea that salvation is merely "fire insurance" came from the church putting a period where the Bible only has a comma. It's not **"For God so loved the world, that he gave his only begotten Son, that whosoever believeth in him should not perish"**—period. So many preachers stop here and emphasize salvation's byproduct of missing hell, and totally ignore God's primary purpose—**"but have everlasting life."** You were saved for intimate relationship with your heavenly Father and His Son.

Jesus came because He loved you! He didn't come as a dutiful Creator under some sense of obligation to rescue His wayward creation. Christ's motivation was pure love, and anyone who loves has a need to be loved in return. God's compassion for you in your lost condition and His passion to restore you to fellowship with Him were combined into a sacrificial love that endured the cross. With the barrier of sin forever removed, you've been freed to receive His love and to love Him in return.

The relationship Adam and Eve lost has now been restored to you. **"Who gave himself for our sins, that he might deliver us from this present evil world, according to the will of God and our Father"** (Gal. 1:4). Jesus didn't just save you from a future evil world (hell); He also delivered you from this present evil world, according to the Father's will. You are now able to walk and talk with Him!

Get to know God!

Thou wilt shew me the path of life: in thy presence is fulness of joy; at thy
right hand there are pleasures for evermore.
PSALM 16:11

Jesus Christ: Whom having not seen, ye love; in whom, though now ye see
him not, yet believing, ye rejoice with joy unspeakable and full of glory.
1 PETER 1:7B-8

True joy and happiness in this life come from your intimacy with God. Knowing Him is eternal life!

FOLLOW ME

Become a disciple of the Lord Jesus Christ! A "disciple" is a learner, someone who follows another. **"If ye continue in my word, then are ye my disciples indeed; And ye shall know the truth, and the truth shall make you free"** (John 8:31-32). Learn what God's Word says, and do what He instructs you to do. As you step out in faith to follow Jesus, the freedom in your life will increase more and more.

Your heart attitude should be, *Lord, I know You love me, and I love You too. Show me what to do and I'll do it! I follow You!* Lay everything out before Him and make no reservations. Recognize that He is God and you're not. Hold nothing back from Him, because He's already given you everything—He laid down His very life for you!

The truth shall make you free. **"Thy word is truth"** (John 17:17). It's only the Word you know and follow that makes you free. You can carry your Bible under your arm and set it beside your bed, but until you put His Word in your heart, it won't do you any good. Meditate (chew on) His Word until it becomes a part of you. Once you believe it to the point of taking action, you'll know the Word intimately. When this knowledge comes, it'll set you free!

YOU'VE CHOSEN WISELY

Welcome to God's family! If you take to heart what I've shared with you and do it, you'll be well on your way to maturity.

I've included for you a helpful list of my teaching materials available that discuss in much greater detail many of the topics I've touched on so far (see **Recommended Materials** in the back of this study guide). God will use them to further deepen your roots and strengthen your foundation. I strongly encourage you to get ahold of them as soon as possible!

Choosing to make the Lord Jesus Christ the center of your life is the greatest decision you'll ever make! I congratulate you for choosing wisely. As your brother in Christ, I wish to leave you with this word from God our Father:

> *But grow in grace, and in the knowledge of our Lord and Saviour Jesus Christ. To him be glory both now and for ever. Amen.*
>
> 2 PETER 3:18

For Further Information:

I strongly suggest you get my teaching "Eternal Life." It expounds much more on your relationship with the Lord.

—— OUTLINE ——

I. God saved you for the purpose of enjoying an intimate relationship with Him from now on.

> *For God so loved the world, that he gave his only begotten Son, that whosoever believeth in him should not perish, but have everlasting life.*
>
> JOHN 3:16

> *And this is life eternal, that they might know thee the only true God, and Jesus Christ, whom thou hast sent.*
>
> JOHN 17:3

A. The idea that salvation is merely "fire insurance" came from the church putting a period where the Bible only has a comma.

B. It's not **"For God so loved the world, that he gave his only begotten Son, that whosoever believeth in him should not perish"**—period.

C. So many preachers stop here and emphasize salvation's byproduct of missing hell, and totally ignore God's primary purpose—**"but have everlasting life."**

D. Jesus didn't come as a dutiful Creator under some sense of obligation to rescue His wayward creation—Christ's motivation was pure love, and anyone who loves has a need to be loved in return.

E. God's compassion for you in your lost condition and His passion to restore you to fellowship with Him were combined into a sacrificial love that endured the cross.

F. With the barrier of sin forever removed, you've been freed to receive His love and to love Him in return.

G. **"Who gave himself for our sins, that he might deliver us from this present evil world, according to the will of God and our Father"** (Gal. 1:4).

H. Jesus didn't just save you from a future evil world (hell); He also delivered you from this present evil world, according to the Father's will.

I. You are now able to walk and talk with Him—get to know God!

> *Thou wilt shew me the path of life: in thy presence is fulness of joy; at thy right hand there are pleasures for evermore.*
>
> PSALM 16:11

> *Jesus Christ: Whom having not seen, ye love; in whom, though now ye see him not, yet believing, ye rejoice with joy unspeakable and full of glory.*
>
> 1 PETER 1:7B-8

J. True joy and happiness in this life come from your intimacy with God.

II. Become a disciple of the Lord Jesus Christ!

   A. A "disciple" is a learner, someone who follows another—**"If ye continue in my word, then are ye my disciples indeed; And ye shall know the truth, and the truth shall make you free"** (John 8:31-32).

   B. As you step out in faith to follow Jesus, the freedom in your life will increase more and more.

   C. Your heart attitude should be, *Lord, I know You love me, and I love You too. Show me what to do and I'll do it! I follow You!*

      i.   Lay everything out before Him and make no reservations.

      ii. Recognize that He is God and you're not.

      iii. Hold nothing back from Him, because He's already given you everything—He laid down His very life for you!

   D. **"Thy word is truth"** (John 17:17)—It's only the Word you know and follow that makes you free.

   E. You can carry your Bible under your arm and set it beside your bed, but until you put His Word in your heart, it won't do you any good.

   F. Meditate (chew on) His Word until it becomes a part of you.

   G. Once you believe it to the point of taking action, you'll know the Word intimately.

   H. When this knowledge comes, it'll set you free!

III. Welcome to God's family!

   A. If you take to heart what I've shared with you and do it, you'll be well on your way to maturity.

   B. Choosing to make the Lord Jesus Christ the center of your life is the greatest decision you'll ever make!

   C. I congratulate you for choosing wisely.

   D. As your brother in Christ, I wish to leave you with this word from God our Father:

      But grow in grace, and in the knowledge of our Lord and Saviour Jesus Christ. To him be glory both now and for ever. Amen.
                                                                    2 PETER 3:18

TEACHER'S
—— GUIDE ——

1. God saved you for the purpose of enjoying an intimate relationship with Him from now on.

> *For God so loved the world, that he gave his only begotten Son, that*
> *whosoever believeth in him should not perish, but have everlasting life.*
> JOHN 3:16

> *And this is life eternal, that they might know thee the only true God, and*
> *Jesus Christ, whom thou hast sent.*
> JOHN 17:3

The idea that salvation is merely "fire insurance" came from the church putting a period where the Bible only has a comma. It's not **"For God so loved the world, that he gave his only begotten Son, that whosoever believeth in him should not perish"**—period. So many preachers stop here and emphasize salvation's byproduct of missing hell, and totally ignore God's primary purpose—**"but have everlasting life."** Jesus didn't come as a dutiful Creator under some sense of obligation to rescue His wayward creation—Christ's motivation was pure love, and anyone who loves has a need to be loved in return. God's compassion for you in your lost condition and His passion to restore you to fellowship with Him were combined into a sacrificial love that endured the cross. With the barrier of sin forever removed, you've been freed to receive His love and to love Him in return. **"Who gave himself for our sins, that he might deliver us from this present evil world, according to the will of God and our Father"** (Gal. 1:4). Jesus didn't just save you from a future evil world (hell); He also delivered you from this present evil world, according to the Father's will. You are now able to walk and talk with Him—get to know God!

> *Thou wilt shew me the path of life: in thy presence is fulness of joy; at thy*
> *right hand there are pleasures for evermore.*
> PSALM 16:11

> *Jesus Christ: Whom having not seen, ye love; in whom, though now ye see*
> *him not, yet believing, ye rejoice with joy unspeakable and full of glory.*
> 1 PETER 1:7B-8

True joy and happiness in this life come from your intimacy with God.

    1a. For what purpose did God save you?
        To enjoy an intimate relationship with Him from now on
    1b. John 3:16 says, "**For God so loved the world, that he gave his only begotten Son, that whosoever believeth in him should not perish, but** _____ _____ _____."
        "Have everlasting life"
    1c. According to John 17:3, what is eternal life?
        Knowing God the Father and Jesus—"that they might know thee the only true God, and Jesus Christ, whom thou hast sent"
    1d. True or false: Jesus came to earth out of a sense of obligation to rescue His wayward creation.
        False

1e. With the barrier of sin forever removed, what has happened to you?
You have been freed to receive His love and to love Him in return

1f. **"Who gave himself for our sins, that he might _____ us from this present _____ world, according to the will of God and our Father"** (Gal. 1:4).
A. Take / stagnant
B. Deliver / evil
C. Buy / average
D. All of the above
E. None of the above
B. "Deliver" / "evil"

2. Become a disciple of the Lord Jesus Christ! A "disciple" is a learner, someone who follows another—**"If ye continue in my word, then are ye my disciples indeed; And ye shall know the truth, and the truth shall make you free"** (John 8:31-32). As you step out in faith to follow Jesus, the freedom in your life will increase more and more. Your heart attitude should be, *Lord, I know You love me, and I love You too. Show me what to do and I'll do it! I follow You!* Lay everything out before Him and make no reservations. Recognize that He is God and you're not. Hold nothing back from Him, because He's already given you everything—He laid down His very life for you! **"Thy word is truth"** (John 17:17)—It's only the Word you know and follow that makes you free. You can carry your Bible under your arm and set it beside your bed, but until you put His Word in your heart, it won't do you any good. Meditate (chew on) His Word until it becomes a part of you. Once you believe it to the point of taking action, you'll know the Word intimately. When this knowledge comes, it'll set you free!

2a. What is a disciple?
A learner, someone who follows another

2b. **"If ye _____ in my word, then are ye my disciples indeed; And ye shall know the _____, and the truth shall make you _____"** (John 8:31-32).
"Continue" / "truth" / "free"

2c. What happens when you step out in faith to follow Jesus?
The freedom in your life will increase

2d. John 17:17 says, "_____ _____ _____ _____."
"Thy word is truth"

2e. True or false: You can carry your Bible under your arm and set it beside your bed, but until you put His Word in your heart, it won't do you any good.
True

3. Welcome to God's family! If you take to heart what I've shared with you and do it, you'll be well on your way to maturity. Choosing to make the Lord Jesus Christ the center of your life is the greatest decision you'll ever make! I congratulate you for choosing wisely. As your brother in Christ, I wish to leave you with this word from God our Father:

> *But grow in grace, and in the knowledge of our Lord and Saviour Jesus Christ. To him be glory both now and for ever. Amen.*
>
> 2 PETER 3:18

3a. Is choosing to make the Lord Jesus Christ the center of your life the greatest decision you'll ever make?
    Yes

3b. Which verse says, **"But grow in grace, and in the knowledge of our Lord and Saviour Jesus Christ. To him be glory both now and for ever. Amen"**?
    2 Peter 3:18

DISCIPLESHIP
—— QUESTIONS ——

1. For what purpose did God save you?

   _____
   _____
   _____

2. John 3:16 says, **"For God so loved the world, that he gave his only begotten Son, that whosoever believeth in him should not perish, but _____ _____ _____."**

3. According to John 17:3, what is eternal life?

   _____
   _____
   _____

4. True or false: Jesus came to earth out of a sense of obligation to rescue His wayward creation.

5. With the barrier of sin forever removed, what has happened to you?

   _____
   _____
   _____

6. **"Who gave himself for our sins, that he might _____ us from this present _____ world, according to the will of God and our Father"** (Gal. 1:4).
   A. Take / stagnant
   B. Deliver / evil
   C. Buy / average
   D. All of the above
   E. None of the above

7. What is a disciple?

   _____
   _____
   _____

8. **"If ye _____ in my word, then are ye my disciples indeed; And ye shall know the _____, and the truth shall make you _____"** (John 8:31-32).

9. What happens when you step out in faith to follow Jesus?

    _____

    _____

    _____

10. John 17:17 says, "_____ _____

    _____ _____."

11. True or false: You can carry your Bible under your arm and set it beside your bed, but until you put His Word in your heart, it won't do you any good.

12. Is choosing to make the Lord Jesus Christ the center of your life the greatest decision you'll ever make?

    _____

    _____

    _____

13. Which verse says, **"But grow in grace, and in the knowledge of our Lord and Saviour Jesus Christ. To him be glory both now and for ever. Amen"**?

    _____

    _____

    _____

ANSWER
—KEY—

1. To enjoy an intimate relationship with Him from now on

2. **"Have everlasting life"**

3. Knowing God the Father and Jesus—**"that they might know thee the only true God, and Jesus Christ, whom thou hast sent"**

4. False

5. You have been freed to receive His love and to love Him in return

6. B. **"Deliver" / "evil"**

7. A learner, someone who follows another

8. **"Continue" / "truth" / "free"**

9. The freedom in your life will increase

10. **"Thy word is truth"**

11. True

12. Yes

13. 2 Peter 3:18

—— SCRIPTURES ——

JOHN 3:16

For God so loved the world, that he gave his only begotten Son, that whosoever believeth in him should not perish, but have everlasting life.

JOHN 17:3

And this is life eternal, that they might know thee the only true God, and Jesus Christ, whom thou hast sent.

GALATIANS 1:4

Who gave himself for our sins, that he might deliver us from this present evil world, according to the will of God and our Father.

PSALM 16:11

Thou wilt shew me the path of life: in thy presence is fulness of joy; at thy right hand there are pleasures for evermore.

1 PETER 1:7-8

That the trial of your faith, being much more precious than of gold that perisheth, though it be tried with fire, might be found unto praise and honour and glory at the appearing of Jesus Christ: [8] Whom having not seen, ye love; in whom, though now ye see him not, yet believing, ye rejoice with joy unspeakable and full of glory.

JOHN 8:31-32

Then said Jesus to those Jews which believed on him, If ye continue in my word, then are ye my disciples indeed; [32] And ye shall know the truth, and the truth shall make you free.

JOHN 17:17

Sanctify them through thy truth: thy word is truth.

2 PETER 3:18

But grow in grace, and in the knowledge of our Lord and Saviour Jesus Christ. To him be glory both now and for ever. Amen.

THE
HOLY
SPIRIT

— INTRODUCTION —

Millions of Christians today have received God's power into their lives through the separate, distinct experience called "the baptism in the Holy Spirit." Wherever you go in the world—Africa, Asia, Europe, North or South America, Australia—these believers are aggressively and effectively advancing the kingdom of God.

I grew up being told that God's miraculous power had ceased on earth with the passing of the early church. This led me to believe that I had received all of the Holy Spirit I could get at salvation. After being saved for many years, I became frustrated with my powerless, defeated Christian life. In desperation, I sought the Lord with all my heart and stumbled into the baptism in the Holy Spirit. This powerful encounter with God revolutionized my entire life!

Today, decades later, my relationship with the Lord is deeper and stronger than ever. I regularly see miracles of every kind, and my teaching ministry literally reaches around the world. None of this would have been possible apart from the supernatural power of the Holy Spirit!

Whether you are newly born again or have been saved for many years, God's Word clearly reveals that the baptism in the Holy Spirit is necessary, standard equipment for living a fruitful and fulfilled Christian life. The Lord Himself commanded, **"Receive ye the Holy Ghost"** (John 20:22). I encourage you to do so today!

EMPOWERED
LIVES

I was born again at eight years old. Our pastor had preached a message on hell in church that morning. Even though I hadn't done many terrible things in my young life, I recognized that I had sinned and fallen short of the glory of God. I knew that "hell" was a place where people who didn't accept Jesus as their Lord and Savior went. This concerned me, so I asked my father about it. He explained God's holiness and how sin separated me from Him. He also told me how God's justice demanded that I go to hell. Then Dad made it clear that Jesus came to forgive my sin and suffer the punishment in my place. I remember praying with my father to receive the Lord right there in my bedroom. Immediately, I felt an inner release as peace flooded my heart.

The next day at school, my friends noticed the change in me before I'd told anyone of my conversion. "What's different with you?" they asked. When I answered that I'd been born again, they immediately started making fun of me for being a Christian. Although these classmates recognized an initial difference at my conversion, subsequent evidence of my faith in Christ was meager at best.

My closest friend from grade school never knew I was a Christian until he saw me recently on television. He'd just gone through an extremely difficult time in life and had reached out to receive the Lord from the absolute end of his rope. While visiting with each other for the first time in over thirty years, he was totally shocked to discover that I'd been a Christian the whole time we were friends together growing up!

My faith simply didn't affect anyone else's life. I prayed six months straight for my father to be healed, but nothing happened. He died when I was twelve. Although I easily overcame temptations others yielded to, the tangible demonstrations of God's power described of believers in the Bible were noticeably absent from my life. Basically, Christianity to me was just the doctrines and beliefs I held inside.

Then, on March 23, 1968, I received the baptism in the Holy Spirit. Something within me exploded, and my understanding of God immediately shot through the roof. It took many years of renewing my mind before I was able to explain to others the things I instantly knew in my spirit. In fact, my mother thought I'd lost my mind because of the sudden, radical, outward transformation of my soul, my thinking, and my actions. My intense, new zeal for God, coupled with a lack of wisdom, even got me kicked out of a few churches. I'd become a fanatic overnight!

You never would've heard of me if I hadn't been baptized in the Holy Spirit. I would have maintained my nominal salvation, surviving until heaven and making practically no eternal impact here on earth. This prior lack of victory and outward manifestation of God's power isn't unique only to me. I've read many, many testimonies of people who experienced the same thing—even in the Bible!

LIKE A DOVE

Jesus Himself did not manifest the power of God until He had been baptized in the Holy Spirit. Angels pronounced Him Lord at His birth, but nothing that typified Christ's ministry—preaching, healing, casting out demons—occurred before the Holy Spirit descended upon Him like a dove.

> *And Jesus, when he was baptized, went up straightway out of the water:*
> *and, lo, the heavens were opened unto him, and he saw the Spirit of God*
> *descending like a dove, and lighting upon him: And lo a voice from heaven,*
> *saying, This is my beloved Son, in whom I am well pleased.*
> MATTHEW 3:16-17

The baptism in the Holy Spirit served as the turning point from natural to supernatural in Christ's life.

Jesus immediately began His ministry after being anointed with the Holy Spirit. The Spirit led Him into the wilderness to confront the devil (Luke 4:1-13). He emerged victorious and then boldly declared in the synagogue of His hometown,

> *The Spirit of the Lord is upon me, because he hath anointed me to preach*
> *the gospel to the poor; he hath sent me to heal the brokenhearted, to preach*
> *deliverance to the captives, and recovering of sight to the blind, to set at*
> *liberty them that are bruised, To preach the acceptable year of the Lord.*
> LUKE 4:18-19

From this point forward, Jesus did what He was anointed to do.

Many times, the Lord admitted His total dependence upon the Father and the Spirit. He did His Father's will as the power of the Holy Spirit flowed in and through Him. Father, Son, and Holy Spirit always worked together in complete cooperation. As a part of this interdependent, triune Godhead, Jesus would not and could not do any miracles until the Holy Spirit had come upon Him.

God never does anything independently of His Spirit. Therefore, welcoming the Holy Spirit into your life is absolutely essential for you to experience the victory and abundance God has provided. If the sinless Son of God had to be baptized in the Holy Spirit before beginning His ministry, how can anyone presume to be an effective Christian without it?

RUCKUS IN THE TEMPLE

The disciples were spineless wimps before receiving the baptism in the Holy Spirit. These men had followed Jesus for three-and-a-half years, observing His miracles, hearing His teaching, and experiencing everyday life with Him. They exhibited weakness, immaturity, carnal-mindedness, and strife. Upon Jesus's arrest, all their promises to stay with Him—to death if need be—went right out the window. They forsook Him and fled for their lives in terror!

Peter denied Jesus three different times just hours after pledging his undying allegiance. His natural strength wilted before a damsel, the high priest's maid, and certain others as they each successively asked, "Aren't you one of Jesus' disciples?" Swearing and taking oaths, he answered, "No, I don't even know the Man!" Peter wept bitterly when he realized what he'd done. He hadn't wanted to deny Christ, but in his own human strength, he was powerless not to do so (Matt. 26:69-75).

Then Peter and the other disciples were baptized in the Holy Spirit. **"And when the day of Pentecost was fully come, they were all with one accord in one place. And suddenly there came a sound from heaven as of a rushing mighty wind. . . . And they were all filled with the Holy Ghost"** (Acts 2:1-2 and 4a). They instantly transformed into powerful witnesses and testified of Jesus with great boldness. Three thousand were saved and water baptized that first day alone (Acts 2:41)!

Shortly thereafter, Peter and John healed a lame man in front of the temple and caused such a ruckus preaching the Gospel that the religious leaders threw them in jail (Acts 3:1-4:3). Thousands more believed their message, so the leaders interrogated Peter and John to find out what was going on.

> *And it came to pass on the morrow, that their rulers, and elders, and scribes,*
> *And Annas the high priest, and Caiaphas, and John, and Alexander, and*
> *as many as were of the kindred of the high priest, were gathered togethor at*
> *Jerusalem. And when they had set them in the midst, they asked, By what*
> *power, or by what name, have ye done this?*
>
> ACTS 4:5-7

Peter boldly confronted the same men who had crucified Jesus!

> *Then Peter, filled with the Holy Ghost, said unto them, Ye rulers of the people,*
> *and elders of Israel, If we this day be examined of the good deed done to the*
> *impotent man, by what means he is made whole; Be it known unto you all,*
> *and to all the people of Israel, that by the name of Jesus Christ of Nazareth,*
> *whom ye crucified, whom God raised from the dead, even by him doth this*
> *man stand here before you whole. This is the stone which was set at nought*
> *of you builders, which is become the head of the corner. Neither is there*
> *salvation in any other: for there is none other name under heaven given*
> *among men, whereby we must be saved.*
>
> ACTS 4:8-12

Peter publicly declared to the entire Jewish leadership that belief in the God of Abraham alone was insufficient for salvation. He clearly told them to believe on the name of Jesus Christ, whom they themselves had killed, or face eternal damnation. Peter left them no avenue of escape: Either accept Jesus or reject Him!

The same men from whom the disciples once fled were now backing down in the face of the disciples' inspired boldness:

> *Now when they saw the boldness of Peter and John, and perceived that they were unlearned and ignorant men, they marvelled; and they took knowledge of them, that they had been with Jesus. And beholding the man which was healed standing with them, they could say nothing against it.*
>									ACTS 4:13-14

The miracle worked by the disciples completely silenced the religious leaders' opposition. What a difference the baptism in the Holy Spirit makes!

CLEAR INSTRUCTIONS

Our Lord's last words to His followers before ascending were clear instructions regarding the Holy Spirit. If your work on earth was done and you were about to turn your entire kingdom over to a small group of people, your last words to them would be very important.

Jesus commanded His disciples not to do anything until they had been baptized in the Holy Spirit.

> *And, being assembled together with them, commanded them that they should not depart from Jerusalem, but wait for the promise of the Father, which, saith he, ye have heard of me. For John truly baptized with water; but ye shall be baptized with the Holy Ghost not many days hence. . . . But ye shall receive power, after that the Holy Ghost is come upon you: and ye shall be witnesses unto me both in Jerusalem, and in all Judaea, and in Samaria, and unto the uttermost part of the earth. And when he had spoken these things, while they beheld, he was taken up; and a cloud received him out of their sight.*
>									ACTS 1:4-5 AND 8-9

Think about how difficult this must have been for the disciples. Jesus had preached God's Word and demonstrated His power on earth like no one ever had before. Due to this, the religious leaders had Him killed and buried. To their natural minds, it appeared that Jesus had been just another man. Yet three days later, He arose from the dead exactly as He prophesied, validating everything He had said. As if that wasn't enough, Jesus spent forty more days on the earth teaching His followers before they personally watched Him ascend to His Father in heaven. These disciples had incredibly good news—news worth shouting from the rooftops—

but Jesus commanded them to sit on it temporarily. Why? They needed the baptism in the Holy Spirit!

It's absolutely wonderful to be born again and forgiven of your sins, but you won't be an effective witness until you have the fullness of the Holy Spirit. When He comes, you'll be able to live in victory and testify in power. The Holy Spirit enables you to more fully experience your salvation and to effectively share with others the awesome things God has done for you.

Many Christians sincerely love God, but they serve Him in their own power because they haven't been baptized in His Spirit. This results in deadness. **"Who also hath made us able ministers of the new testament; not of the letter, but of the spirit: for the letter killeth, but the spirit giveth life"** (2 Cor. 3:6). When believers try to minister out of their own carnal knowledge and ability—even when they say and do the right thing—it just doesn't carry any spiritual weight. So much of the deadness in the church today stems from believers attempting to minister without Holy Spirit empowerment.

Jesus Christ Himself testifies and ministers His life through witnesses empowered by the Holy Spirit. Your Spirit-energized words and deeds will carry weight to positively impact other people's lives for the kingdom of God. The Holy Spirit is the One who will help you experience the promised life of victory and abundance. If both Jesus and the early believers needed to be baptized in the Holy Spirit in order to live powerful Christian lives, so do you and I today!

— OUTLINE —

I. Jesus Himself did not manifest the power of God until He had been baptized in the Holy Spirit.

   A. Angels pronounced Him Lord at His birth, but nothing that typified Christ's ministry—preaching, healing, casting out demons—occurred before the Holy Spirit descended upon Him like a dove.

   > *And Jesus, when he was baptized, went up straightway out of the water: and, lo, the heavens were opened unto him, and he saw the Spirit of God descending like a dove, and lighting upon him: And lo a voice from heaven, saying, This is my beloved Son, in whom I am well pleased.*
   > MATTHEW 3:16-17

   B. Jesus immediately began His ministry after being anointed with the Holy Spirit.

   C. Many times, the Lord admitted His total dependence upon the Father and the Spirit.

   D. He did His Father's will as the power of the Holy Spirit flowed in and through Him—Father, Son, and Holy Spirit always worked together in complete cooperation.

   E. God never does anything independently of His Spirit.

   F. Therefore, welcoming the Holy Spirit into your life is absolutely essential for you to experience the victory and abundance God has provided.

II. The disciples were spineless wimps before receiving the baptism in the Holy Spirit.

   A. These men had followed Jesus for three-and-a-half years, observing His miracles, hearing His teaching, and experiencing everyday life with Him.

   B. They exhibited weakness, immaturity, carnal-mindedness, and strife.

   C. Then the disciples were baptized in the Holy Spirit—**"And when the day of Pentecost was fully come, they were all with one accord in one place. And suddenly there came a sound from heaven as of a rushing mighty wind. . . . And they were all filled with the Holy Ghost"** (Acts 2:1-2 and 4a).

   D. They instantly transformed into powerful witnesses and testified of Jesus with great boldness.

   E. Shortly thereafter, Peter and John healed a lame man in front of the temple and caused such a ruckus preaching the Gospel that the religious leaders threw them in jail (Acts 3:1-4:3).

   F. Thousands more believed their message, so the leaders interrogated Peter and John to find out what was going on.

> *And it came to pass on the morrow, that their rulers, and elders, and scribes, And Annas the high priest, and Caiaphas, and John, and Alexander, and as many as were of the kindred of the high priest, were gathered togethor at Jerusalem. And when they had set them in the midst, they asked, By what power, or by what name, have ye done this?*
>
> ACTS 4:5-7

G. Peter boldly confronted the same men who had crucified Jesus!

> *Then Peter, filled with the Holy Ghost, said unto them, Ye rulers of the people, and elders of Israel, If we this day be examined of the good deed done to the impotent man, by what means he is made whole; Be it known unto you all, and to all the people of Israel, that by the name of Jesus Christ of Nazareth, whom ye crucified, whom God raised from the dead, even by him doth this man stand here before you whole. This is the stone which was set at nought of you builders, which is become the head of the corner. Neither is there salvation in any other: for there is none other name under heaven given among men, whereby we must be saved.*
>
> ACTS 4:8-12

H. Peter left them no avenue of escape: Either accept Jesus or reject Him!

I. The same men from whom the disciples once fled were now backing down in the face of the disciples' inspired boldness:

> *Now when they saw the boldness of Peter and John, and perceived that they were unlearned and ignorant men, they marvelled; and they took knowledge of them, that they had been with Jesus. And beholding the man which was healed standing with them, they could say nothing against it.*
>
> ACTS 4:13-14

J. The miracle worked by the disciples completely silenced the religious leaders' opposition.

K. What a difference the baptism in the Holy Spirit makes!

III. Our Lord's last words to His followers before ascending were clear instructions regarding the Holy Spirit.

A. Jesus commanded His disciples not to do anything until they had been baptized in the Holy Spirit.

> *And, being assembled together with them, commanded them that they should not depart from Jerusalem, but wait for the promise of the Father, which, saith he, ye have heard of me. For John truly baptized with water; but ye shall be baptized with the Holy Ghost not many days hence. . . . But ye shall receive power, after that the Holy Ghost is come upon you: and ye shall be witnesses unto me both in Jerusalem, and in all Judaea, and in Samaria, and unto the uttermost part of the earth. And when he had spoken these things, while they beheld, he was taken up; and a cloud received him out of their sight.*
>
> ACTS 1:4-5 AND 8-9

B. Think about how difficult this must have been for the disciples.

C. These disciples had incredibly good news—news worth shouting from the rooftops—but Jesus commanded them to sit on it temporarily.

D. Why? They needed the baptism in the Holy Spirit!

E. It's absolutely wonderful to be born again and forgiven of your sins, but you won't be an effective witness until you have the fullness of the Holy Spirit.

F. The Holy Spirit enables you to more fully experience your salvation and to effectively share with others the awesome things God has done for you.

G. Many Christians sincerely love God, but they serve Him in their own power because they haven't been baptized in His Spirit—this results in deadness.

H. **"Who also hath made us able ministers of the new testament; not of the letter, but of the spirit: for the letter killeth, but the spirit giveth life"** (2 Cor. 3:6).

I. When believers try to minister out of their own carnal knowledge and ability—even when they say and do the right thing—it just doesn't carry any spiritual weight.

J. Jesus Christ Himself testifies and ministers His life through witnesses empowered by the Holy Spirit.

K. Your Spirit-energized words and deeds will carry weight to positively impact other people's lives for the kingdom of God.

L. If both Jesus and the early believers needed to be baptized in the Holy Spirit in order to live powerful Christian lives, so do you and I today!

TEACHER'S
GUIDE

1. Jesus Himself did not manifest the power of God until He had been baptized in the Holy Spirit. Angels pronounced Him Lord at His birth, but nothing that typified Christ's ministry—preaching, healing, casting out demons—occurred before the Holy Spirit descended upon Him like a dove.

> *And Jesus, when he was baptized, went up straightway out of the water: and, lo, the heavens were opened unto him, and he saw the Spirit of God descending like a dove, and lighting upon him: And lo a voice from heaven, saying, This is my beloved Son, in whom I am well pleased.*
>
> MATTHEW 3:16-17

Jesus immediately began His ministry after being anointed with the Holy Spirit. Many times, the Lord admitted His total dependence upon the Father and the Spirit. He did His Father's will as the power of the Holy Spirit flowed in and through Him—Father, Son, and Holy Spirit always worked together in complete cooperation. God never does anything independently of His Spirit. Therefore, welcoming the Holy Spirit into your life is absolutely essential for you to experience the victory and abundance God has provided.

1a. True or false: Jesus Himself did not manifest the power of God until He had been baptized in the Holy Spirit.
True

1b. Matthew 3:16-17 says, **"And Jesus, when he was baptized, went up straightway out of the water: and, lo, the heavens were opened unto him, and he saw the** _____ **descending like a dove, and lighting upon him: And lo a voice from heaven, saying, This is my beloved Son, in whom I am well pleased."**
"Spirit of God"

1c. When did Jesus begin His ministry?
Immediately after being anointed with the Holy Spirit

1d. God never does anything how?
A. Wisely
B. Independently of His Spirit
C. Without money
D. All of the above
E. None of the above
B. Independently of His Spirit

1e. Is welcoming the Holy Spirit into your life absolutely essential for you to experience the victory and abundance God has provided?
Yes

2. The disciples were spineless wimps before receiving the baptism in the Holy Spirit. These men had followed Jesus for three-and-a-half years, observing His miracles, hearing His teaching, and experiencing everyday life with Him. They exhibited weakness, immaturity, carnal-mindedness, and strife. Then the disciples were baptized in the Holy Spirit—**"And when the day of Pentecost was fully come, they were all with one accord in one place. And suddenly there came a sound from heaven as of a rushing mighty wind. . . . And they were all filled with the Holy Ghost"** (Acts 2:1-2 and 4a). They instantly transformed into powerful witnesses and testified of Jesus with great boldness. Shortly thereafter, Peter and John healed a lame man in front of the temple and caused such a ruckus preaching the Gospel that the religious leaders threw them in jail (Acts 3:1-4:3). Thousands more believed their message, so the leaders interrogated Peter and John to find out what was going on.

> *And it came to pass on the morrow, that their rulers, and elders, and scribes, And Annas the high priest, and Caiaphas, and John, and Alexander, and as many as were of the kindred of the high priest, were gathered togethor at Jerusalem. And when they had set them in the midst, they asked, By what power, or by what name, have ye done this?*
>
> ACTS 4:5-7

Peter boldly confronted the same men who had crucified Jesus!

> *Then Peter, filled with the Holy Ghost, said unto them, Ye rulers of the people, and elders of Israel, If we this day be examined of the good deed done to the impotent man, by what means he is made whole; Be it known unto you all, and to all the people of Israel, that by the name of Jesus Christ of Nazareth, whom ye crucified, whom God raised from the dead, even by him doth this man stand here before you whole. This is the stone which was set at nought of you builders, which is become the head of the corner. Neither is there salvation in any other: for there is none other name under heaven given among men, whereby we must be saved.*
>
> ACTS 4:8-12

Peter left them no avenue of escape: Either accept Jesus or reject Him! The same men from whom the disciples once fled were now backing down in the face of the disciples' inspired boldness:

> *Now when they saw the boldness of Peter and John, and perceived that they were unlearned and ignorant men, they marvelled; and they took knowledge of them, that they had been with Jesus. And beholding the man which was healed standing with them, they could say nothing against it.*
>
> ACTS 4:13-14

The miracle worked by the disciples completely silenced the religious leaders' opposition. What a difference the baptism in the Holy Spirit makes!

   2a. What happened after the disciples were baptized in the Holy Spirit?
   They were instantly transformed into powerful witnesses and testified of Jesus with great boldness

2b. True or false: After healing the lame man in front of the temple, Peter ran away from the religious leaders (Acts 4:5-14).
False

2c. What choice did Peter give them?
Either accept Jesus or reject Him!

2d. What did the miracle that the disciples worked do (Acts 4:13-14)?
It completely silenced the religious leaders' opposition

3. Our Lord's last words to His followers before ascending were clear instructions regarding the Holy Spirit. Jesus commanded His disciples not to do anything until they had been baptized in the Holy Spirit.

> *And, being assembled together with them, commanded them that they should not depart from Jerusalem, but wait for the promise of the Father, which, saith he, ye have heard of me. For John truly baptized with water; but ye shall be baptized with the Holy Ghost not many days hence. . . . But ye shall receive power, after that the Holy Ghost is come upon you: and ye shall be witnesses unto me both in Jerusalem, and in all Judaea, and in Samaria, and unto the uttermost part of the earth. And when he had spoken these things, while they beheld, he was taken up; and a cloud received him out of their sight.*
> ACTS 1:4-5 AND 8-9

Think about how difficult this must have been for the disciples. These disciples had incredibly good news—news worth shouting from the rooftops—but Jesus commanded them to sit on it temporarily. Why? They needed the baptism in the Holy Spirit! It's absolutely wonderful to be born again and forgiven of your sins, but you won't be an effective witness until you have the fullness of the Holy Spirit. The Holy Spirit enables you to more fully experience your salvation and to effectively share with others the awesome things God has done for you. Many Christians sincerely love God, but they serve Him in their own power because they haven't been baptized in His Spirit—this results in deadness. **"Who also hath made us able ministers of the new testament; not of the letter, but of the spirit: for the letter killeth, but the spirit giveth life"** (2 Cor. 3:6). When believers try to minister out of their own carnal knowledge and ability—even when they say and do the right thing—it just doesn't carry any spiritual weight. Jesus Christ Himself testifies and ministers His life through witnesses empowered by the Holy Spirit. Your Spirit-energized words and deeds will carry weight to positively impact other people's lives for the kingdom of God. If both Jesus and the early believers needed to be baptized in the Holy Spirit in order to live powerful Christian lives, so do you and I today!

3a. At His ascension (Acts 1:4-5 and 8-9), what command did Jesus give His disciples?
  A. To preach the Gospel in King James English
  B. To immediately go and preach
  C. Not to do anything until they had been baptized in the Holy Spirit
  D. All of the above
  E. None of the above
  C. Not to do anything until they had been baptized in the Holy Spirit

3b. What will make you an effective witness?
Having the fullness of the Holy Spirit

3c. Many Christians sincerely love God, but they serve Him in their own
_____ because they haven't been baptized in His Spirit—this results
in _____.
Power / deadness

3d. When believers try to minister out of their own carnal knowledge and ability—even
when they say and do the right thing—does it carry any spiritual weight?
No

3e. What will your Spirit-energized words and deeds do?
Positively impact other people's lives for the kingdom of God

3f. True or false: If both Jesus and the early believers needed to be baptized in the Holy
Spirit in order to live powerful Christian lives, so do you and I today!
True

DISCIPLESHIP
—— QUESTIONS ——

1. True or false: Jesus Himself did not manifest the power of God until He had been baptized in the Holy Spirit.

   _____
   _____
   _____

2. Matthew 3:16-17 says, **"And Jesus, when he was baptized, went up straightway out of the water: and, lo, the heavens were opened unto him, and he saw the** _____ _____ _____ **descending like a dove, and lighting upon him: And lo a voice from heaven, saying, This is my beloved Son, in whom I am well pleased."**

3. When did Jesus begin His ministry?

   _____
   _____
   _____

4. God never does anything how?
   A. Wisely
   B. Independently of His Spirit
   C. Without money
   D. All of the above
   E. None of the above

5. Is welcoming the Holy Spirit into your life absolutely essential for you to experience the victory and abundance God has provided?

   _____
   _____
   _____

6. What happened after the disciples were baptized in the Holy Spirit?

   _____
   _____
   _____

7. True or false: After healing the lame man in front of the temple, Peter ran away from the religious leaders (Acts 4:5-14).

8. What choice did Peter give them?

_____

_____

_____

9. What did the miracle that the disciples worked do (Acts 4:13-14)?

_____

_____

_____

10. At His ascension (Acts 1:4-5 and 8-9), what command did Jesus give His disciples?
    A. To preach the Gospel in King James English
    B. To immediately go and preach
    C. Not to do anything until they had been baptized in the Holy Spirit
    D. All of the above
    E. None of the above

11. What will make you an effective witness?

_____

_____

_____

12. Many Christians sincerely love God, but they serve Him in their own _____ because they haven't been baptized in His Spirit—this results in _____.

13. When believers try to minister out of their own carnal knowledge and ability—even when they say and do the right thing—does it carry any spiritual weight?

_____

_____

_____

14. What will your Spirit-energized words and deeds do?

_____

_____

_____

15. True or false: If both Jesus and the early believers needed to be baptized in the Holy Spirit in order to live powerful Christian lives, so do you and I today!

ANSWER
——KEY——

1. True

2. **"Spirit of God"**

3. Immediately after being anointed with the Holy Spirit

4. B. Independently of His Spirit

5. Yes

6. They were instantly transformed into powerful witnesses and testified of Jesus with great boldness

7. False

8. Either accept Jesus or reject Him!

9. It completely silenced the religious leaders' opposition

10. C. Not to do anything until they had been baptized in the Holy Spirit

11. Having the fullness of the Holy Spirit

12. Power / deadness

13. No

14. Positively impact other people's lives for the kingdom of God

15. True

— SCRIPTURES —

MATTHEW 3:16-17

And Jesus, when he was baptized, went up straightway out of the water: and, lo, the heavens were opened unto him, and he saw the Spirit of God descending like a dove, and lighting upon him: [17] And lo a voice from heaven, saying, This is my beloved Son, in whom I am well pleased.

LUKE 4:1-13

And Jesus being full of the Holy Ghost returned from Jordan, and was led by the Spirit into the wilderness, [2] Being forty days tempted of the devil. And in those days he did eat nothing: and when they were ended, he afterward hungered. [3] And the devil said unto him, If thou be the Son of God, command this stone that it be made bread. [4] And Jesus answered him, saying, It is written, That man shall not live by bread alone, but by every word of God. [5] And the devil, taking him up into an high mountain, shewed unto him all the kingdoms of the world in a moment of time. [6] And the devil said unto him, All this power will I give thee, and the glory of them: for that is delivered unto me; and to whomsoever I will I give it. [7] If thou therefore wilt worship me, all shall be thine. [8] And Jesus answered and said unto him, Get thee behind me, Satan: for it is written, Thou shalt worship the Lord thy God, and him only shalt thou serve. [9] And he brought him to Jerusalem, and set him on a pinnacle of the temple, and said unto him, If thou be the Son of God, cast thyself down from hence: [10] For it is written, He shall give his angels charge over thee, to keep thee: [11] And in their hands they shall bear thee up, lest at any time thou dash thy foot against a stone. [12] And Jesus answering said unto him, It is said, Thou shalt not tempt the Lord thy God. [13] And when the devil had ended all the temptation, he departed from him for a season.

LUKE 4:18-19

The Spirit of the Lord is upon me, because he hath anointed me to preach the gospel to the poor; he hath sent me to heal the brokenhearted, to preach deliverance to the captives, and recovering of sight to the blind, to set at liberty them that are bruised, [19] To preach the acceptable year of the Lord.

MATTHEW 26:69-75

Now Peter sat without in the palace: and a damsel came unto him, saying, Thou also wast with Jesus of Galilee. [70] But he denied before them all, saying, I know not what thou sayest. [71] And when he was gone out into the porch, another maid saw him, and said unto them that were there, This fellow was also with Jesus of Nazareth. [72] And again he denied with an oath, I do not know the man. [73] And after a while came unto him they that stood by, and said to Peter, Surely thou also art one of them; for thy speech bewrayeth thee. [74] Then began he to curse and to swear, saying, I know not the man. And immediately the cock crew. [75] And Peter remembered the word of Jesus, which said unto him, Before the cock crow, thou shalt deny me thrice. And he went out, and wept bitterly.

ACTS 2:1-2

And when the day of Pentecost was fully come, they were all with one accord in one place. [2] And suddenly there came a sound from heaven as of a rushing mighty wind, and it filled all the house where they were sitting.

ACTS 2:4

And they were all filled with the Holy Ghost, and began to speak with other tongues, as the Spirit gave them utterance.

ACTS 2:41

Then they that gladly received his word were baptized: and the same day there were added unto them about three thousand souls.

ACTS 3:1-4:3

Now Peter and John went up together into the temple at the hour of prayer, being the ninth hour. [2] And a certain man lame from his mother's womb was carried, whom they laid daily at the gate of the temple which is called Beautiful, to ask alms of them that entered into the temple; [3] Who seeing Peter and John about to go into the temple asked an alms. [4] And Peter, fastening his eyes upon him with John, said, Look on us. [5] And he gave heed unto them, expecting to receive something of them. [6] Then Peter said, Silver and gold have I none; but such as I have give I thee: In the name of Jesus Christ of Nazareth rise up and walk. [7] And he took him by the right hand, and lifted him up: and immediately his feet and ankle bones received strength. [8] And he leaping up stood, and walked, and entered with them into the temple, walking, and leaping, and praising God. [9] And all the people saw him walking and praising God: [10] And they knew that it was he which sat for alms at the Beautiful gate of the temple: and they were filled with wonder and amazement at that which had happened unto him. [11] And as the lame man which was healed held Peter and John, all the people ran together unto them in the porch that is called Solomon's, greatly wondering. [12] And when Peter saw it, he answered unto the people, Ye men of Israel, why marvel ye at this? or why look ye so earnestly on us, as though by our own power or holiness we had made this man to walk? [13] The God of Abraham, and of Isaac, and of Jacob, the God of our fathers, hath glorified his Son Jesus; whom ye delivered up, and denied him in the presence of Pilate, when he was determined to let him go. [14] But ye denied the Holy One and the Just, and desired a murderer to be granted unto you; [15] And killed the Prince of life, whom God hath raised from the dead; whereof we are witnesses. [16] And his name through faith in his name hath made this man strong, whom ye see and know: yea, the faith which is by him hath given him this perfect soundness in the presence of you all. [17] And now, brethren, I wot that through ignorance ye did it, as did also your rulers. [18] But those things, which God before had shewed by the mouth of all his prophets, that Christ should suffer, he hath so fulfilled. [19] Repent ye therefore, and be converted, that your sins may be blotted out, when the times of refreshing shall come from the presence of the Lord. [20] And he shall send Jesus Christ, which before was preached unto you: [21] Whom the heaven must receive until the times of restitution of all things, which God hath spoken by the mouth of all his holy prophets since the world began. [22] For Moses truly said unto the fathers, A prophet shall the Lord your God raise up unto you of your brethren, like unto me; him shall ye hear in all things whatsoever he shall say unto you. [23] And it shall come to pass, that every soul, which will not hear that prophet, shall be destroyed from among the people. [24] Yea, and all the prophets from Samuel and those that follow after, as many as have spoken, have likewise foretold of these days. [25] Ye are the children of the prophets, and of the covenant which God made with our fathers, saying unto Abraham, And in thy seed shall all the kindreds of the earth be blessed. [26] Unto you first God, having raised up his Son Jesus, sent him to bless you, in turning away every one of you from his iniquities.
[1] And as they spake unto the people, the priests, and the captain of the temple, and the Sadducees, came upon them, [2] Being grieved that they taught the people, and preached through Jesus the resurrection from the dead. [3] And they laid hands on them, and put them in hold unto the next day: for it was now eventide.

ACTS 4:5-14

And it came to pass on the morrow, that their rulers, and elders, and scribes, [6] And Annas the high priest, and Caiaphas, and John, and Alexander, and as many as were of the kindred of the high priest, were gathered together at Jerusalem. [7] And when they had set them in the midst, they asked, By what power, or by what name, have ye done this? [8] Then Peter, filled with the Holy Ghost, said unto them, Ye rulers of the people, and elders of Israel, [9] If we this day be examined of the good deed done to the impotent man, by what means he is made whole; [10] Be it known unto you all, and to all the people of Israel, that by the name of Jesus Christ of Nazareth, whom ye crucified, whom God raised from the dead, even by him doth this man stand here before you whole. [11] This is the stone which was set at nought of you builders, which is become the head of the corner. [12] Neither is there salvation in any other: for there is none other name under heaven given among men, whereby we must be saved. [13] Now when they saw the boldness of Peter and John, and perceived that they were unlearned and ignorant men, they marvelled; and they took knowledge of them, that they had been with Jesus. [14] And beholding the man which was healed standing with them, they could say nothing against it.

ACTS 1:4-5

And, being assembled together with them, commanded them that they should not depart from Jerusalem, but wait for the promise of the Father, which, saith he, ye have heard of me. [5] For John truly baptized with water; but ye shall be baptized with the Holy Ghost not many days hence.

ACTS 1:8-9

But ye shall receive power, after that the Holy Ghost is come upon you: and ye shall be witnesses unto me both in Jerusalem, and in all Judaea, and in Samaria, and unto the uttermost part of the earth. [9] And when he had spoken these things, while they beheld, he was taken up; and a cloud received him out of their sight.

2 CORINTHIANS 3:6

Who also hath made us able ministers of the new testament; not of the letter, but of the spirit: for the letter killeth, but the spirit giveth life.

BAPTIZED
IN THE
HOLY SPIRIT

If you believe the Word of God, you cannot dispute the existence of a baptism in the Holy Spirit. Speaking of Jesus, John the Baptist said, **"I indeed baptize you with water unto repentance: but he that cometh after me is mightier than I, whose shoes I am not worthy to bear: he shall baptize you with the Holy Ghost, and with fire"** (Matt. 3:11). Christ was baptized in the Holy Spirit (Matt. 3:16, Mark 1:10, and Luke 3:22). The early apostles, including Paul, were baptized in the Holy Spirit (Acts 2:1-4 and 9:17-18). Whenever people were born again in the book of Acts, they also received the baptism in the Holy Spirit soon thereafter.

Many Christians claim that the baptism in the Holy Spirit comes automatically at salvation. **"No man can come to me, except the Father which hath sent me draw him: and I will raise him up at the last day"** (John 6:44). They recognize the Spirit's work in drawing people to God and assume that they get all of the Holy Spirit they can the moment they're born again. Although it's true that they have the Holy Spirit once they're saved, that doesn't mean they've been baptized in Him!

RIVERS OF LIVING WATER

It's one thing to have the Holy Spirit and quite another for the Holy Spirit to have you! There are major differences between having the Holy Spirit present in your life and having the Holy Spirit in control of your life. Spiritually speaking, it's night and day.

Jesus told His disciples,

> *And I will pray the Father, and he shall give you another Comforter, that he may abide with you for ever; Even the Spirit of truth; whom the world cannot receive, because it seeth him not, neither knoweth him: but ye know him; for he dwelleth with you, and shall be in you.*
>
> JOHN 14:16-17

Prior to Jesus's resurrection, the Holy Spirit couldn't be received the way I'm discussing with you. He was present ***with*** the disciples and worked through them (as evidenced by the miracles they did), but He wasn't ***in*** them. This was because the fullness of the Holy Spirit couldn't be received until after Christ had ascended back to heaven in glory.

When the Holy Spirit is in you, rivers of life flow out from your innermost being.

> *Jesus stood and cried, saying, If any man thirst, let him come unto me, and drink. He that believeth on me, as the scripture hath said, out of his belly shall flow rivers of living water. (But this spake he of the Spirit, which they that believe on him should receive: for the Holy Ghost was not yet given; because that Jesus was not yet glorified.)*
>
> JOHN 7:37-39

Not just a trickle or a cupful, not even a well you have to pump, but *rivers* of living water will bubble out from within you like an artesian spring!

Jesus promised His disciples that the Holy Spirit who had been with them would one day be in them. That day arrived shortly after His ascension.

> *And when the day of Pentecost was fully come, they were all with one accord in one place. And suddenly there came a sound from heaven as of a rushing mighty wind, and it filled all the house where they were sitting. And there appeared unto them cloven tongues like as of fire, and it sat upon each of them. And they were all filled with the Holy Ghost, and began to speak with other tongues, as the Spirit gave them utterance.*
>
> ACTS 2:1-4

THE POWER SOURCE

Those who don't believe that the baptism in the Holy Spirit is a second, separate experience from salvation erroneously teach that God's miraculous power ceased with the passing of the first apostles. They don't believe in the gifts of the Spirit, speaking in tongues, or casting out demons—nor living in victory over sickness, disease, and poverty. They believe that if you see any of these miracles occurring today that God Himself did in the Bible, it's the work of the devil. Something's wrong with this theology!

The Holy Spirit is the power Source! Reject Him and you won't see miracles, healings, demons cast out, or speaking in tongues. Accept Him by receiving the baptism in the Holy Spirit, and you open yourself to God's supernatural power working in all these wonderful ways—but you must receive the Source in order to have His power.

A SEPARATE EXPERIENCE

The Bible makes it clear that the baptism in the Holy Spirit is a separate experience from salvation. The only way you can miss this is if you have some kind of religious prejudice against it. In Acts 8, Philip went to Samaria and preached Christ. Seeing the miracles he did, many believed and were water baptized (Acts 8:5-12). When the church in Jerusalem heard what had happened, they sent Peter and John to check it out. They arrived, saw those who had been saved, and then laid hands on them to receive the baptism in the Holy Spirit (Acts 8:14-17).

Some people assume, "You aren't really saved until you're baptized in the Holy Spirit!" Acts 8 soundly refutes this. The Samaritans had received God's Word, were born again, and had been water baptized. If they had died before being baptized in the Holy Spirit, they would've been ushered into the very presence of the Lord Himself. Salvation saves and the baptism in the Holy Spirit empowers!

Certain disciples at Ephesus also demonstrate this truth.

> *And it came to pass, that, while Apollos was at Corinth, Paul having passed through the upper coasts came to Ephesus: and finding certain disciples, He said unto them, Have ye received the Holy Ghost since ye believed? And they said unto him, We have not so much as heard whether there be any Holy Ghost.*
>
> ACTS 19:1-2

Apollos had been zealously preaching Jesus wherever he went (Acts 18:24-25). However, he had left the company of the disciples before Christ resurrected, so they didn't know about the baptism in the Holy Spirit either. Aquila and Priscilla had to take him aside and explain the way of God to him more accurately (Acts 18:26). Before this, Apollos had already made some converts in Ephesus, whom Paul found some time later. When he asked "Have you received the Holy Spirit," they answered, **"We have not so much as heard whether there be any Holy Ghost"** (Acts 19:2). Sounds like many Christians today!

I was raised in church, but no one ever told me I could be supernaturally empowered by the Holy Spirit. I didn't know He wanted to come and work miracles through me. Our church didn't believe in that. We were saved but stuck! Besides winning others to the Lord and singing "When we all get to heaven," there just wasn't anything else to look forward to in our Christian lives. I was ignorant of the fact that God had provided a victorious, abundant life on earth for me.

Apollos' converts believed in Jesus but didn't know that the Holy Spirit had been sent to anoint them as their Lord had been anointed. Paul picked up where Apollos left off and shared with these Ephesian believers how they could receive God's power into their lives. **"And when Paul had laid his hands upon them, the Holy Ghost came on them; and they spake with tongues, and prophesied"** (Acts 19:6).

IMPACT YOUR WORLD!

Millions of people alive today can attest to this separate, distinct work of the Holy Spirit in their lives after salvation. Although many born-again Christians in Western countries deny this experience, the majority of believers in the rest of the world have welcomed the baptism in the Holy Spirit!

Africa, Asia, and South America have experienced some of the greatest outpourings we've seen in recent times. Miracles regularly happen and churches sometimes number into the tens, even hundreds, of thousands. The vast majority of believers involved in these outpourings have received the baptism in the Holy Spirit with speaking in tongues.

Across the body of Christ worldwide, the parts that are experiencing the most growth are those who believe in the baptism in the Holy Spirit. Most traditional, denominational churches that fight against this gift have either stagnated or are suffering serious decline. Spirit-baptized believers are progressing in the Christian life, doing most of the effective evangelism and making the biggest impact for the advancing kingdom of God.

Do you want to be where God's power is moving? Are you hungry to experience excitement and life? Do you long to join the winning side? You'll find all this and more among believers who have been baptized in the Holy Spirit!

—— OUTLINE ——

I. If you believe the Word of God, you cannot dispute the existence of a baptism in the Holy Spirit.

    A. Speaking of Jesus, John the Baptist said, **"I indeed baptize you with water unto repentance: but he that cometh after me is mightier than I, whose shoes I am not worthy to bear: he shall baptize you with the Holy Ghost, and with fire"** (Matt. 3:11).

    B. Christ was baptized in the Holy Spirit (Matt. 3:16, Mark 1:10, and Luke 3:22).

    C. The early apostles, including Paul, were baptized in the Holy Spirit (Acts 2:1-4 and 9:17-18).

    D. Whenever people were born again in the book of Acts, they also received the baptism in the Holy Spirit soon thereafter.

    E. Many Christians claim that the baptism in the Holy Spirit comes automatically at salvation—**"No man can come to me, except the Father which hath sent me draw him: and I will raise him up at the last day"** (John 6:44).

    F. They recognize the Spirit's work in drawing people to God and assume that they get all of the Holy Spirit they can the moment they're born again.

    G. Although it's true that they have the Holy Spirit once they're saved, that doesn't mean they've been baptized in Him!

II. ***It's one thing to have the Holy Spirit and quite another for the Holy Spirit to have you!***

    A. There are major differences between having the Holy Spirit present in your life and having the Holy Spirit in control of your life.

    B. Jesus told His disciples,

> *And I will pray the Father, and he shall give you another Comforter, that he may abide with you for ever; Even the Spirit of truth; whom the world cannot receive, because it seeth him not, neither knoweth him: but ye know him; for he dwelleth with you, and shall be in you.*
>
> JOHN 14:16-17

    C. Prior to Jesus's resurrection, the Holy Spirit couldn't be received the way I'm discussing with you.

    D. He was present ***with*** the disciples and worked through them (as evidenced by the miracles they did), but He wasn't ***in*** them.

    E. When the Holy Spirit is in you, rivers of life flow out from your innermost being.

Jesus stood and cried, saying, If any man thirst, let him come unto me, and drink. He that believeth on me, as the scripture hath said, out of his belly shall flow rivers of living water. (But this spake he of the Spirit, which they that believe on him should receive: for the Holy Ghost was not yet given; because that Jesus was not yet glorified.)

JOHN 7:37-39

F. Jesus promised His disciples that the Holy Spirit who had been with them would one day be in them—that day arrived shortly after His ascension.

And when the day of Pentecost was fully come, they were all with one accord in one place. And suddenly there came a sound from heaven as of a rushing mighty wind, and it filled all the house where they were sitting. And there appeared unto them cloven tongues like as of fire, and it sat upon each of them. And they were all filled with the Holy Ghost, and began to speak with other tongues, as the Spirit gave them utterance.

ACTS 2:1-4

III. Those who don't believe that the baptism in the Holy Spirit is a second, separate experience from salvation, erroneously teach that God's miraculous power ceased with the passing of the first apostles.

A. They don't believe in the gifts of the Spirit, speaking in tongues, or casting out demons—nor living in victory over sickness, disease, and poverty.

B. They believe that if you see any of these miracles occurring today that God Himself did in the Bible, it's the work of the devil.

C. Something's wrong with this theology!

D. The Holy Spirit is the power Source!

E. Reject Him and you won't see miracles, healings, demons cast out, or speaking in tongues.

F. Accept Him by receiving the baptism in the Holy Spirit, and you open yourself to God's supernatural power working in all these wonderful ways—but you must receive the Source in order to have His power.

IV. The Bible makes it clear that the baptism in the Holy Spirit is a separate experience from salvation.

A. The only way you can miss this is if you have some kind of religious prejudice against it.

B. Some people assume, "You aren't really saved until you're baptized in the Holy Spirit!"

C. Acts 8 soundly refutes this.

D. Salvation saves and the baptism in the Holy Spirit empowers!

E. Certain disciples at Ephesus also demonstrate this truth.

And it came to pass, that, while Apollos was at Corinth, Paul having passed through the upper coasts came to Ephesus: and finding certain disciples, He said unto them, Have ye received the Holy Ghost since ye believed? And they said unto him, We have not so much as heard whether there be any Holy Ghost.

ACTS 19:1-2

F. Apollos had been zealously preaching Jesus wherever he went (Acts 18:24-25); however, he had left the company of the disciples before Christ resurrected, so they didn't know about the baptism in the Holy Spirit either.

G. Before this, Apollos had already made some converts in Ephesus, whom Paul found some time later.

H. Paul picked up where Apollos left off and shared with these Ephesian believers how they could receive God's power into their lives—**"And when Paul had laid his hands upon them, the Holy Ghost came on them; and they spake with tongues, and prophesied"** (Acts 19:6).

V. Millions of people alive today can attest to this separate, distinct work of the Holy Spirit in their lives after salvation.

A. Although many born-again Christians in Western countries deny this experience, the majority of believers in the rest of the world have welcomed the baptism in the Holy Spirit!

B. Across the body of Christ worldwide, the parts that are experiencing the most growth are those who believe in the baptism in the Holy Spirit.

C. Most traditional, denominational churches that fight against this gift have either stagnated or are suffering serious decline.

D. Spirit-baptized believers are progressing in the Christian life, doing most of the effective evangelism and making the biggest impact for the advancing kingdom of God.

i. Do you want to be where God's power is moving?

ii. Are you hungry to experience excitement and life?

iii. Do you long to join the winning side?

E. You'll find all this and more among believers who have been baptized in the Holy Spirit!

TEACHER'S
GUIDE

1. If you believe the Word of God, you cannot dispute the existence of a baptism in the Holy Spirit. Speaking of Jesus, John the Baptist said, **"I indeed baptize you with water unto repentance: but he that cometh after me is mightier than I, whose shoes I am not worthy to bear: he shall baptize you with the Holy Ghost, and with fire"** (Matt. 3:11). Christ was baptized in the Holy Spirit (Matt. 3:16, Mark 1:10, and Luke 3:22). The early apostles, including Paul, were baptized in the Holy Spirit (Acts 2:1-4 and 9:17-18). Whenever people were born again in the book of Acts, they also received the baptism in the Holy Spirit soon thereafter. Many Christians claim that the baptism in the Holy Spirit comes automatically at salvation—**"No man can come to me, except the Father which hath sent me draw him: and I will raise him up at the last day"** (John 6:44). They recognize the Spirit's work in drawing people to God and assume that they get all of the Holy Spirit they can the moment they're born again. Although it's true that they have the Holy Spirit once they're saved, that doesn't mean they've been baptized in Him!

    1a. True or false: If you believe the Word of God, you cannot dispute the existence of a baptism in the Holy Spirit.
       True
    1b. Speaking of Jesus, John the Baptist said, **"I indeed baptize you with water unto repentance: but he that cometh after me is mightier than I, whose shoes I am not worthy to bear: he shall baptize you with the _____, and with fire"** (Matt. 3:11).
       "Holy Ghost"
    1c. What do many Christians claim regarding the baptism of the Holy Spirit?
       That it comes automatically at salvation
    1d. Although it's true they have the Holy Spirit once they're saved, does that mean they've been baptized in Him?
       No

2. *It's one thing to have the Holy Spirit and quite another for the Holy Spirit to have you!*
There are major differences between having the Holy Spirit present in your life and having the Holy Spirit in control of your life. Jesus told His disciples,

> *And I will pray the Father, and he shall give you another Comforter, that he may abide with you for ever; Even the Spirit of truth; whom the world cannot receive, because it seeth him not, neither knoweth him: but ye know him; for he dwelleth with you, and shall be in you.*
>
> JOHN 14:16-17

Prior to Jesus's resurrection, the Holy Spirit couldn't be received the way I'm discussing with you. He was present **with** the disciples and worked through them (as evidenced by the miracles they did), but He wasn't **in** them. When the Holy Spirit is in you, rivers of life flow out from your innermost being.

> *Jesus stood and cried, saying, If any man thirst, let him come unto me, and drink. He that believeth on me, as the scripture hath said, out of his belly shall flow rivers of living water. (But this spake he of the Spirit, which they that believe on him should receive: for the Holy Ghost was not yet given; because that Jesus was not yet glorified.)*
>
> JOHN 7:37-39

Jesus promised His disciples that the Holy Spirit who had been with them would one day be in them—that day arrived shortly after His ascension.

> *And when the day of Pentecost was fully come, they were all with one accord in one place. And suddenly there came a sound from heaven as of a rushing mighty wind, and it filled all the house where they were sitting. And there appeared unto them cloven tongues like as of fire, and it sat upon each of them. And they were all filled with the Holy Ghost, and began to speak with other tongues, as the Spirit gave them utterance.*
>
> ACTS 2:1-4

2a. There are major differences between having the Holy Spirit present in your life and what?
   Having the Holy Spirit in control of your life
2b. Prior to Jesus' resurrection, what couldn't happen?
   A. The Holy Spirit couldn't work at all
   B. You couldn't speak in other languages
   C. The Holy Spirit couldn't be received the way I'm discussing with you
   D. All of the above
   E. None of the above
   C. The Holy Spirit couldn't be received the way I'm discussing with you
2c. John 7:37-39 says, **"Jesus stood and cried, saying, If any man thirst, let him come unto me, and drink. He that believeth on me, as the scripture hath said, out of his belly shall flow_____ _____**
   _____ _____. (But this spake he of the Spirit, which they that believe on him should receive: for the Holy Ghost was not yet given; because that Jesus was not yet glorified.)"
   "Rivers of living water"

3. Those who don't believe that the baptism in the Holy Spirit is a second, separate experience from salvation, erroneously teach that God's miraculous power ceased with the passing of the first apostles. They don't believe in the gifts of the Spirit, speaking in tongues, or casting out demons—nor living in victory over sickness, disease, and poverty. They believe that if you see any of these miracles occurring today that God Himself did in the Bible, it's the work of the devil. Something's wrong with this theology! The Holy Spirit is the power Source! Reject Him and you won't see miracles, healings, demons cast out, or speaking in tongues. Accept Him by receiving the baptism in the Holy Spirit, and you open yourself to God's supernatural power working in all these wonderful ways—but you must receive the Source in order to have His power.

    3a. True or false: Those who don't believe that the baptism in the Holy Spirit is a second, separate experience from salvation, correctly teach that God's miraculous power ceased with the passing of the first apostles.
False

    3b. What happens when you accept the Holy Spirit by receiving the baptism of the Holy Spirit?
You open yourself to God's supernatural power in all these wonderful ways (i.e., miracles, healings, demons cast out, speaking in tongues)

    3c. What must you do in order to have His power?
You must receive the Source

4. The Bible makes it clear that the baptism in the Holy Spirit is a separate experience from salvation. The only way you can miss this is if you have some kind of religious prejudice against it. Some people assume, "You aren't really saved until you're baptized in the Holy Spirit!" Acts 8 soundly refutes this. Salvation saves and the baptism in the Holy Spirit empowers! Certain disciples at Ephesus also demonstrate this truth.

> *And it came to pass, that, while Apollos was at Corinth, Paul having passed through the upper coasts came to Ephesus: and finding certain disciples, He said unto them, Have ye received the Holy Ghost since ye believed? And they said unto him, We have not so much as heard whether there be any Holy Ghost.*
>
> ACTS 19:1-2

Apollos had been zealously preaching Jesus wherever he went (Acts 18:24-25); however, he had left the company of the disciples before Christ resurrected, so they didn't know about the baptism in the Holy Spirit either. Before this, Apollos had already made some converts in Ephesus, whom Paul found some time later. Paul picked up where Apollos left off and shared with these Ephesian believers how they could receive God's power into their lives—**"And when Paul had laid his hands upon them, the Holy Ghost came on them; and they spake with tongues, and prophesied"** (Acts 19:6).

4a. The Bible makes it clear that the baptism in the Holy Spirit is what?
   A. A separate experience from salvation
   B. Absolutely necessary for salvation
   C. Not for us today
   D. All of the above
   E. None of the above
   A. A separate experience from salvation
4b. What chapter of the Bible soundly refutes the idea that you aren't really saved until you're baptized in the Holy Spirit?
   Acts 8
4c. Salvation _____ and the baptism in the Holy Spirit _____!
   Saves / empowers
4d. What did Paul do for the Ephesian believers in Acts 19?
   He picked up where Apollos left off and shared with them how they could receive God's power into their lives

5. Millions of people alive today can attest to this separate, distinct work of the Holy Spirit in their lives after salvation. Although many born-again Christians in Western countries deny this experience, the majority of believers in the rest of the world have welcomed the baptism in the Holy Spirit! Across the body of Christ worldwide, the parts that are experiencing the most growth are those who believe in the baptism in the Holy Spirit. Most traditional, denominational churches that fight against this gift have either stagnated or are suffering serious decline. Spirit-baptized believers are progressing in the Christian life, doing most of the effective evangelism and making the biggest impact for the advancing kingdom of God. Do you want to be where God's power is moving? Are you hungry to experience excitement and life? Do you long to join the winning side? You'll find all this and more among believers who have been baptized in the Holy Spirit!

    5a. Across the body of Christ worldwide, what is happening to the parts that believe in the baptism of the Holy Spirit?
       They are experiencing the most growth
    5b. What has happened to the churches that fight this gift?
       They have stagnated or are suffering serious decline
    5c. True or false: Spirit-baptized believers are progressing in the Christian life, doing most of the effective evangelism and making the biggest impact for the advancing kingdom of God.
       True

DISCIPLESHIP
——— QUESTIONS ———

1. True or false: If you believe the Word of God, you cannot dispute the existence of a baptism in the Holy Spirit.

2. Speaking of Jesus, John the Baptist said, **"I indeed baptize you with water unto repentance: but he that cometh after me is mightier than I, whose shoes I am not worthy to bear: he shall baptize you with the**_____ _____**, and with fire"** (Matt. 3:11).

3. What do many Christians claim regarding the baptism of the Holy Spirit?
    _____
    _____
    _____

4. Although it's true they have the Holy Spirit once they're saved, does that mean they've been baptized in Him?
    _____
    _____
    _____

5. There are major differences between having the Holy Spirit present in your life and what?
    _____
    _____
    _____

6. Prior to Jesus' resurrection, what couldn't happen?
    A. The Holy Spirit couldn't work at all
    B. You couldn't speak in other languages
    C. The Holy Spirit couldn't be received the way I'm discussing with you
    D. All of the above
    E. None of the above

7. John 7:37-39 says, **"Jesus stood and cried, saying, If any man thirst, let him come unto me, and drink. He that believeth on me, as the scripture hath said, out of his belly shall flow** _____
    _____ _____**. (But this spake he of the Spirit, which they that believe on him should receive: for the Holy Ghost was not yet given; because that Jesus was not yet glorified.)"**

8. True or false: Those who don't believe that the baptism in the Holy Spirit is a second, separate experience from salvation, correctly teach that God's miraculous power ceased with the passing of the first apostles.

9. What happens when you accept the Holy Spirit by receiving the baptism of the Holy Spirit?

10. What must you do in order to have His power?

11. The Bible makes it clear that the baptism in the Holy Spirit is what?
    A. A separate experience from salvation
    B. Absolutely necessary for salvation
    C. Not for us today
    D. All of the above
    E. None of the above

12. What chapter of the Bible soundly refutes the idea that you aren't really saved until you're baptized in the Holy Spirit?

13. Salvation _____ and the baptism in the Holy Spirit _____!

14. What did Paul do for the Ephesian believers in Acts 19?

15. Across the body of Christ worldwide, what is happening to the parts that believe in the baptism of the Holy Spirit?

16. What has happened to the churches that fight this gift?

_____
_____
_____

17. True or false: Spirit-baptized believers are progressing in the Christian life, doing most of the effective evangelism and making the biggest impact for the advancing kingdom of God.

ANSWER
—KEY—

1. True

2. **"Holy Ghost"**

3. That it comes automatically at salvation

4. No

5. Having the Holy Spirit in control of your life

6. C. The Holy Spirit couldn't be received the way I'm discussing with you

7. **"Rivers of living water"**

8. False

9. You open yourself to God's supernatural power in all these wonderful ways (i.e., miracles, healings, demons cast out, speaking in tongues)

10. You must receive the Source

11. A. A separate experience from salvation

12. Acts 8

13. Saves / empowers

14. He picked up where Apollos left off and shared with them how they could receive God's power into their lives

15. They are experiencing the most growth

16. They have stagnated or are suffering serious decline

17. True

—— SCRIPTURES ——

MATTHEW 3:11

I indeed baptize you with water unto repentance: but he that cometh after me is mightier than I, whose shoes I am not worthy to bear: he shall baptize you with the Holy Ghost, and with fire.

MATTHEW 3:16

And Jesus, when he was baptized, went up straightway out of the water: and, lo, the heavens were opened unto him, and he saw the Spirit of God descending like a dove, and lighting upon him.

MARK 1:10

And straightway coming up out of the water, he saw the heavens opened, and the Spirit like a dove descending upon him.

LUKE 3:22

And the Holy Ghost descended in a bodily shape like a dove upon him, and a voice came from heaven, which said, Thou art my beloved Son; in thee I am well pleased.

ACTS 2:1-4

And when the day of Pentecost was fully come, they were all with one accord in one place. [2] And suddenly there came a sound from heaven as of a rushing mighty wind, and it filled all the house where they were sitting. [3] And there appeared unto them cloven tongues like as of fire, and it sat upon each of them. [4] And they were all filled with the Holy Ghost, and began to speak with other tongues, as the Spirit gave them utterance.

ACTS 9:17-18

And Ananias went his way, and entered into the house; and putting his hands on him said, Brother Saul, the Lord, even Jesus, that appeared unto thee in the way as thou camest, hath sent me, that thou mightest receive thy sight, and be filled with the Holy Ghost. [18] And immediately there fell from his eyes as it had been scales: and he received sight forthwith, and arose, and was baptized.

JOHN 6:44

No man can come to me, except the Father which hath sent me draw him: and I will raise him up at the last day.

JOHN 14:16-17

And I will pray the Father, and he shall give you another Comforter, that he may abide with you for ever; [17] Even the Spirit of truth; whom the world cannot receive, because it seeth him not, neither knoweth him: but ye know him; for he dwelleth with you, and shall be in you.

JOHN 7:37-39

In the last day, that great day of the feast, Jesus stood and cried, saying, If any man thirst, let him come unto me, and drink. [38] He that believeth on me, as the scripture hath said, out of his belly shall flow rivers of living water. [39] (But this spake he of the Spirit, which they that believe on him should receive: for the Holy Ghost was not yet given; because that Jesus was not yet glorified.)

ACTS 8:5-12

Then Philip went down to the city of Samaria, and preached Christ unto them. [6] And the people with one accord gave heed unto those things which Philip spake, hearing and seeing the miracles which he did. [7] For unclean spirits, crying with loud voice, came out of many that were possessed with them: and many taken with palsies, and that were lame, were healed. [8] And there was great joy in that city. [9] But there was a certain man, called Simon, which beforetime in the same city used sorcery, and bewitched the people of Samaria, giving out that himself was some great one: [10] To whom they all gave heed, from the least to the greatest, saying, This man is the great power of God. [11] And to him they had regard, because that of long time he had bewitched them with sorceries. [12] But when they believed Philip preaching the things concerning the kingdom of God, and the name of Jesus Christ, they were baptized, both men and women.

ACTS 8:14-17

Now when the apostles which were at Jerusalem heard that Samaria had received the word of God, they sent unto them Peter and John: [15] Who, when they were come down, prayed for them, that they might receive the Holy Ghost: [16] (For as yet he was fallen upon none of them: only they were baptized in the name of the Lord Jesus.) [17] Then laid they their hands on them, and they received the Holy Ghost.

ACTS 19:1-2

And it came to pass, that, while Apollos was at Corinth, Paul having passed through the upper coasts came to Ephesus: and finding certain disciples, [2] He said unto them, Have ye received the Holy Ghost since ye believed? And they said unto him, We have not so much as heard whether there be any Holy Ghost.

ACTS 18:24-26

And a certain Jew named Apollos, born at Alexandria, an eloquent man, and mighty in the scriptures, came to Ephesus. [25] This man was instructed in the way of the Lord; and being fervent in the spirit, he spake and taught diligently the things of the Lord, knowing only the baptism of John. [26] And he began to speak boldly in the synagogue: whom when Aquila and Priscilla had heard, they took him unto them, and expounded unto him the way of God more perfectly.

ACTS 19:6

And when Paul had laid his hands upon them, the Holy Ghost came on them; and they spake with tongues, and prophesied.

THE
FULL
PACKAGE

Jesus often referred to the Holy Spirit as the "Comforter." He'll function in your life many different ways:

The Holy Spirit will abide with you forever. **"And I will pray the Father, and he shall give you another Comforter, that he may abide with you for ever"** (John 14:16). Wherever you go, whatever you do, God Himself will be with you!

The Holy Spirit will comfort you through challenges and difficulties. **"Who comforteth us in all our tribulation, that we may be able to comfort them which are in any trouble, by the comfort wherewith we ourselves are comforted of God"** (2 Cor. 1:4). He'll also enable you to minister God's comfort to others.

The Holy Spirit will be your Teacher. **"But the Comforter, which is the Holy Ghost, whom the Father will send in my name, he shall teach you all things, and bring all things to your remembrance, whatsoever I have said unto you"** (John 14:26). He'll also remind you of everything the Lord has said.

The Spirit of truth will testify to you of Jesus. **"But when the Comforter is come, whom I will send unto you from the Father, even the Spirit of truth, which proceedeth from the Father, he shall testify of me: And ye also shall bear witness, because ye have been with me from the beginning"** (John 15:26-27). He'll also help you bear witness of Jesus to others.

"IT'S BETTER THAT I GO"

It's to your advantage that Jesus is in heaven, and the Holy Spirit is on earth. **"Nevertheless I tell you the truth; It is expedient for you that I go away: for if I go not away, the Comforter will not come unto you; but if I depart, I will send him unto you"** (John 16:7). Jesus could only be in one place at a time when He walked the earth as a man. Now, through His Spirit, He can be with every believer all the time!

The Holy Spirit will convict and convince. **"And when he is come, he will reprove the world of sin, and of righteousness, and of judgment: Of sin, because they believe not on me; Of righteousness, because I go to my Father, and ye see me no more; Of judgment, because the prince of this world is judged"** (John 16:8-11). He convicts you of not trusting Jesus. He convinces you that you're righteous in Christ. And the devil, who constantly hurls condemnation and lies at you, is judged.

The Holy Spirit will guide you into all truth. **"I have yet many things to say unto you, but ye cannot bear them now. Howbeit when he, the Spirit of truth, is come, he will guide you into all truth: for he shall not speak of himself; but whatsoever he shall hear, that shall he speak: and he will shew you things to come"** (John 16:12-13). The Spirit of truth will progressively share Jesus's words with you as you're mature enough to handle them. He'll even reveal things yet to come!

The Holy Spirit will glorify Jesus. **"He shall glorify me: for he shall receive of mine, and shall shew it unto you"** (John 16:14). He'll receive things from the Lord and show them to you.

God's power will flood into you as you're baptized in Him. **"But ye shall receive power, after that the Holy Ghost is come upon you: and ye shall be witnesses unto me both in Jerusalem, and in all Judaea, and in Samaria, and unto the uttermost part of the earth"** (Acts 1:8). Wherever you go, you'll be an effective witness!

ESSENTIAL, NOT OPTIONAL!

In light of all these awesome benefits, I urge you to accept the fact that the baptism in the Holy Spirit is not merely optional but essential. Receive His power so you can fully experience the Comforter!

The baptism in the Holy Spirit makes God's power available to you. Although you're not automatically transformed into a victorious Christian, you'll experience increasing victory as you draw out His power by faith. This is why some people who have received the baptism in the Holy Spirit don't exhibit more victory in their lives. God's power is available to them, but they haven't drawn it out. Those who reject the baptism in the Holy Spirit deny themselves access to His power. You must have received the Source in order to access His power!

Some Christians may have been baptized in the Holy Spirit without realizing it. They are wonderful people who don't speak in tongues or believe in a distinct experience with the Holy Spirit, yet they clearly exhibit all of the other characteristics of someone who has received the baptism. Often, with many of them, there was a time in their lives when they came to the end of themselves. They cried out to the Lord for help, asking for more of Him. After yielding, they had a miraculous encounter with God. Now, whether they're aware of what they received or not, if the encounter actually included being baptized in the Holy Spirit, they can now speak in tongues anytime they want just by exercising their faith to do so.

God intends for you to have His full package! Some theologians from the 1800s and early 1900s taught about a second, separate experience with the Lord but didn't teach on speaking in tongues. They believed there had to be an enduing of power from on high, but they failed to embrace the accompanying miracles. Why receive only part of God's gift? Why not receive it all? Your loving heavenly Father cared enough to give you the baptism in the Holy Spirit. Honor Him by receiving the full package!

—— OUTLINE ——

I. The Holy Spirit will function in your life many different ways:

A. The Holy Spirit will abide with you forever.

   i. **"And I will pray the Father, and he shall give you another Comforter, that he may abide with you for ever"** (John 14:16).

   ii. Wherever you go, whatever you do, God Himself will be with you!

B. The Holy Spirit will comfort you through challenges and difficulties.

   i. **"Who comforteth us in all our tribulation, that we may be able to comfort them which are in any trouble, by the comfort wherewith we ourselves are comforted of God"** (2 Cor. 1:4).

   ii. He'll also enable you to minister God's comfort to others.

C. The Holy Spirit will be your Teacher.

   i. **"But the Comforter, which is the Holy Ghost, whom the Father will send in my name, he shall teach you all things, and bring all things to your remembrance, whatsoever I have said unto you"** (John 14:26).

   ii. He'll also remind you of everything the Lord has said.

D. The Spirit of truth will testify to you of Jesus.

   i. **"But when the Comforter is come, whom I will send unto you from the Father, even the Spirit of truth, which proceedeth from the Father, he shall testify of me: And ye also shall bear witness, because ye have been with me from the beginning"** (John 15:26-27).

   ii. He'll also help you bear witness of Jesus to others.

II. It's to your advantage that Jesus is in heaven, and the Holy Spirit is on earth— **"Nevertheless I tell you the truth; It is expedient for you that I go away: for if I go not away, the Comforter will not come unto you; but if I depart, I will send him unto you"** (John 16:7).

A. Jesus could only be in one place at a time when He walked the earth as a man—now, through His Spirit, He can be with every believer all the time!

B. The Holy Spirit will convict and convince: **"And when he is come, he will reprove the world of sin, and of righteousness, and of judgment: Of sin, because they believe not on me; Of righteousness, because I go to my Father, and ye see me no more; Of judgment, because the prince of this world is judged"** (John 16:8-11).

      i.   He convicts you of not trusting Jesus.

      ii. He convinces you that you're righteous in Christ.

      iii. And the devil, who constantly hurls condemnation and lies at you, is judged.

C. The Holy Spirit will guide you into all truth: **"I have yet many things to say unto you, but ye cannot bear them now. Howbeit when he, the Spirit of truth, is come, he will guide you into all truth: for he shall not speak of himself; but whatsoever he shall hear, that shall he speak: and he will shew you things to come"** (John 16:12-13).

      i.   The Spirit of truth will progressively share Jesus's words with you as you're mature enough to handle them.

D. The Holy Spirit will glorify Jesus: **"He shall glorify me: for he shall receive of mine, and shall shew it unto you"** (John 16:14).

      i.   He'll receive things from the Lord and show them to you.

E. God's power will flood into you as you're baptized in Him: **"But ye shall receive power, after that the Holy Ghost is come upon you: and ye shall be witnesses unto me both in Jerusalem, and in all Judaea, and in Samaria, and unto the uttermost part of the earth"** (Acts 1:8).

III. In light of all these awesome benefits, I urge you to accept the fact that the baptism in the Holy Spirit is not merely optional but essential.

A. The baptism in the Holy Spirit makes God's power available to you.

B. Although you're not automatically transformed into a victorious Christian, you'll experience increasing victory as you draw out His power by faith.

C. Those who reject the baptism in the Holy Spirit deny themselves access to His power.

D. Some Christians may have been baptized in the Holy Spirit without realizing it.

E. They are wonderful people who don't speak in tongues or believe in a distinct experience with the Holy Spirit, yet they clearly exhibit all of the other characteristics of someone who has received the baptism.

F. God intends for you to have His full package!

      i.   Why receive only part of God's gift?

      ii. Why not receive it all?

G. Your loving heavenly Father cared enough to give you the baptism in the Holy Spirit— honor Him by receiving the full package!

TEACHER'S GUIDE

1. The Holy Spirit will function in your life many different ways: The Holy Spirit will abide with you forever. **"And I will pray the Father, and he shall give you another Comforter, that he may abide with you for ever"** (John 14:16). Wherever you go, whatever you do, God Himself will be with you! The Holy Spirit will comfort you through challenges and difficulties. **"Who comforteth us in all our tribulation, that we may be able to comfort them which are in any trouble, by the comfort wherewith we ourselves are comforted of God"** (2 Cor. 1:4). He'll also enable you to minister God's comfort to others. The Holy Spirit will be your Teacher. **"But the Comforter, which is the Holy Ghost, whom the Father will send in my name, he shall teach you all things, and bring all things to your remembrance, whatsoever I have said unto you"** (John 14:26). He'll also remind you of everything the Lord has said. The Spirit of truth will testify to you of Jesus. **"But when the Comforter is come, whom I will send unto you from the Father, even the Spirit of truth, which proceedeth from the Father, he shall testify of me: And ye also shall bear witness, because ye have been with me from the beginning"** (John 15:26-27). He'll also help you bear witness of Jesus to others.

1a. True or false: The Holy Spirit will abide with you for as long as you attend church faithfully.
False

1b. **"And I will pray the Father, and he shall give you another** _____, **that he may abide with you for ever"** (John 14:16).
"Comforter"

1c. According to 2 Corinthians 1:4, what two things will the Holy Spirit do for you?
He will comfort you through challenges and difficulties, and He'll enable you to minister God's comfort to others

1d. What verse tells you that the Holy Spirit **"shall teach you all things, and bring all things to your remembrance, whatsoever I have said unto you"**?
John 14:26

1e. John 15:26-27 says, **"But when the Comforter is come, whom I will send unto you from the Father, even the Spirit of truth, which proceedeth from the Father, he shall testify of** _____ **: And ye also shall bear** _____ **, because ye have been with me from the beginning."**
A. Love / fruit
B. Me / witness
C. Truth / crosses
D. All of the above
E. None of the above
B. "Me" / "witness"

2. It's to your advantage that Jesus is in heaven, and the Holy Spirit is on earth—**"Nevertheless I tell you the truth; It is expedient for you that I go away: for if I go not away, the Comforter will not come unto you; but if I depart, I will send him unto you"** (John 16:7). Jesus could only be in one place at a time when He walked the earth as a man—now, through His Spirit, He can be with every believer all the time! The Holy Spirit will convict and convince: **"And when he is come, he will reprove the world of sin, and of righteousness, and of judgment: Of sin, because they believe not on me; Of righteousness, because I go to my Father, and ye see me no more; Of judgment, because the prince of this world is judged"** (John 16:8-11). He convicts you of not trusting Jesus. He convinces you that you're righteous in Christ. And the devil, who constantly hurls condemnation and lies at you, is judged. The Holy Spirit will guide you into all truth: **"I have yet many things to say unto you, but ye cannot bear them now. Howbeit when he, the Spirit of truth, is come, he will guide you into all truth: for he shall not speak of himself; but whatsoever he shall hear, that shall he speak: and he will shew you things to come"** (John 16:12-13). The Spirit of truth will progressively share Jesus's words with you as you're mature enough to handle them. The Holy Spirit will glorify Jesus: **"He shall glorify me: for he shall receive of mine, and shall shew it unto you"** (John 16:14). He'll receive things from the Lord and show them to you. God's power will flood into you as you're baptized in Him: **"But ye shall receive power, after that the Holy Ghost is come upon you: and ye shall be witnesses unto me both in Jerusalem, and in all Judaea, and in Samaria, and unto the uttermost part of the earth"** (Acts 1:8).

2a. What is the lesson being taught by John 16:7?
   That it's to your advantage that Jesus is in heaven, and the Holy Spirit is on earth

2b. Why is it advantageous that Jesus went to heaven and sent you His Spirit?
   Because Jesus could only be in one place at a time when He walked the earth as a man—now, through His Spirit, He can be with every believer all the time

2c. True or false: The Holy Spirit convicts you of not trusting Jesus.
   True

2d. True or false: The Holy Spirit convinces you that you're righteous in Christ.
   True

2e. True or false: The devil, who constantly hurls condemnation and lies at you, may be judged.
   False

2f. John 16:12-13 says, **"I have yet many things to say unto you, but ye cannot bear them now. Howbeit when he, the Spirit of truth, is come, will
   _____ you into all _____: for he shall not speak of himself; but whatsoever he shall hear, that shall he speak: and he will shew you
   _____ _____ _____ _____."**
   "Guide" / "truth" / "things to come"

3. In light of all these awesome benefits, I urge you to accept the fact that the baptism in the Holy Spirit is not merely optional but essential. The baptism in the Holy Spirit makes God's power available to you. Although you're not automatically transformed into a victorious Christian, you'll experience increasing victory as you draw out His power by faith. Those who reject the baptism in the Holy Spirit deny themselves access to His power. Some Christians may have been baptized in the Holy Spirit without realizing it. They are wonderful people who don't speak in tongues or believe in a distinct experience with the Holy Spirit, yet they clearly exhibit all of the other characteristics of someone who has received the baptism. God intends for you to have His full package! Why receive only part of God's gift? Why not receive it all? Your loving heavenly Father cared enough to give you the baptism in the Holy Spirit—honor Him by receiving the full package!

3a. The baptism in the Holy Spirit is not merely…
   A. Needed but received
   B. For the early church but for you today
   C. Recommended but preached
   D. All of the above
   E. None of the above
   E. None of the above
3b. Are you automatically transformed into a victorious Christian when you receive the baptism of the Holy Spirit?
   No
3c. Is it honoring God to receive the full package He has given?
   Yes

DISCIPLESHIP
—— QUESTIONS ——

1. True or false: The Holy Spirit will abide with you for as long as you attend church faithfully.

2. **"And I will pray the Father, and he shall give you another _____, that he may abide with you for ever"** (John 14:16).

3. According to 2 Corinthians 1:4, what two things will the Holy Spirit do for you?
   _____
   _____
   _____

4. What verse tells you that the Holy Spirit **"shall teach you all things, and bring all things to your remembrance, whatsoever I have said unto you"**?
   _____
   _____
   _____

5. John 15:26-27 says, **"But when the Comforter is come, whom I will send unto you from the Father, even the Spirit of truth, which proceedeth from the Father, he shall testify of _____: And ye also shall bear _____, because ye have been with me from the beginning."**
   A. Love / fruit
   B. Me / witness
   C. Truth / crosses
   D. All of the above
   E. None of the above

6. What is the lesson being taught by John 16:7?
   _____
   _____
   _____

7. Why is it advantageous that Jesus went to heaven and sent you His Spirit?
   _____
   _____
   _____

8. True or false: The Holy Spirit convicts you of not trusting Jesus.

9. True or false: The Holy Spirit convinces you that you're righteous in Christ.

10. True or false: The devil, who constantly hurls condemnation and lies at you, may be judged.

11. John 16:12-13 says, **"I have yet many things to say unto you, but ye cannot bear them now. Howbeit when he, the Spirit of truth, is come, he will _____ you into all _____: for he shall not speak of himself; but whatsoever he shall hear, that shall he speak: and he will shew you _____ _____ _____."**

12. The baptism in the Holy Spirit is not merely…
    A. Needed but received
    B. For the early church but for you today
    C. Recommended but preached
    D. All of the above
    E. None of the above

13. Are you automatically transformed into a victorious Christian when you receive the baptism of the Holy Spirit?

    _____
    _____
    _____

14. Is it honoring God to receive the full package He has given?

    _____
    _____
    _____

ANSWER
—KEY—

1. False

2. **"Comforter"**

3. He will comfort you through challenges and difficulties, and He'll enable you to minister God's comfort to others

4. John 14:26

5. B. **"Me" / "witness"**

6. That it's to your advantage that Jesus is in heaven, and the Holy Spirit is on earth

7. Because Jesus could only be in one place at a time when He walked the earth as a man—now, through His Spirit, He can be with every believer all the time

8. True

9. True

10. False

11. **"Guide" / "truth" / "things to come"**

12. E. None of the above

13. No

14. Yes

—— SCRIPTURES ——

JOHN 14:16

And I will pray the Father, and he shall give you another Comforter, that he may abide with you for ever.

2 CORINTHIANS 1:4

Who comforteth us in all our tribulation, that we may be able to comfort them which are in any trouble, by the comfort wherewith we ourselves are comforted of God.

JOHN 14:26

But the Comforter, which is the Holy Ghost, whom the Father will send in my name, he shall teach you all things, and bring all things to your remembrance, whatsoever I have said unto you.

JOHN 15:26-27

But when the Comforter is come, whom I will send unto you from the Father, even the Spirit of truth, which proceedeth from the Father, he shall testify of me: [27] And ye also shall bear witness, because ye have been with me from the beginning.

JOHN 16:7-14

Nevertheless I tell you the truth; It is expedient for you that I go away: for if I go not away, the Comforter will not come unto you; but if I depart, I will send him unto you. [8] And when he is come, he will reprove the world of sin, and of righteousness, and of judgment: [9] Of sin, because they believe not on me; [10] Of righteousness, because I go to my Father, and ye see me no more; [11] Of judgment, because the prince of this world is judged. [12] I have yet many things to say unto you, but ye cannot bear them now. [13] Howbeit when he, the Spirit of truth, is come, he will guide you into all truth: for he shall not speak of himself; but whatsoever he shall hear, that shall he speak: and he will shew you things to come. [14] He shall glorify me: for he shall receive of mine, and shall shew it unto you.

ACTS 1:8

But ye shall receive power, after that the Holy Ghost is come upon you: and ye shall be witnesses unto me both in Jerusalem, and in all Judaea, and in Samaria, and unto the uttermost part of the earth.

RECEIVE
HIM
TODAY

God wants you baptized in the Holy Spirit! His longing to fill, control, and empower you far surpasses your desire to be filled, controlled, and empowered. In fact, the Holy Spirit has been eagerly waiting for you to open your heart and invite Him in. If you're ready to ask in faith, why not receive Him today?

Some groups erroneously teach that you must "travail" and wait on God to receive this experience. They believe that God will baptize you whenever He wants to and that you have no control over it. This idea is based upon a misinterpretation of Acts 1:4-5, which says,

> *And, being assembled together with them, commanded them that they should not depart from Jerusalem, but wait for the promise of the Father, which, saith he, ye have heard of me. For John truly baptized with water; but ye shall be baptized with the Holy Ghost not many days hence.*

Jesus commanded the disciples to wait for the baptism because the Holy Spirit had not yet been poured out upon the earth. **"And when the day of Pentecost was fully come, they were all with one accord in one place. . . . And they were all filled with the Holy Ghost"** (Acts 2:1 and 4). Pentecost was God's appointed time to pour out the Holy Spirit. Since He's already been given, there's no need to wait!

While seeking the baptism in the Holy Spirit, I was told I had to cleanse myself before I could receive. As instructed, I wrote out every sin I could think of in my misguided effort to get "clean enough." Religious logic had deceived me into thinking "a jar full of rocks must be emptied before being filled with water" and "the Holy Spirit won't fill a dirty vessel." Hogwash!

The baptism in the Holy Spirit is a *gift*, not something you can earn by travail or holiness (Luke 11:13). If you could rid yourself of all the sin in your life and be perfect before receiving the Holy Spirit, you wouldn't need Him! He's the One who will give you the power to be set free from lusts, habits, addictions, and desires. You can be delivered from anything when you receive and draw on the power of the Holy Spirit.

WHOLEHEARTED DESIRE

You need to desire the baptism in the Holy Spirit wholeheartedly. If you are persuaded and hungry, receiving can be as simple as praying a prayer. However, some people have been led to do so before they were really ready. Occasionally, someone needs a period of time to grow in their hunger and desire to receive. Where are you today? Are you persuaded and hungry for the baptism? Do you wholeheartedly desire to invite the Holy Spirit into your life?

Personally, I was desperate for the baptism in the Holy Spirit. I thought I had to pursue God and then wait for it. This misunderstanding only increased my growing hunger to receive. Then, when the baptism came, it was spectacular! Since this was something I'd longed for and sought after, I didn't just forget about it after speaking in tongues once or twice. Over the years, I've cherished this awesome gift from God. Without His power, I wouldn't be living in the victory and abundance I enjoy today—for which I'm eternally grateful!

Are you ready to commit yourself to the Holy Spirit without reservation? Are you hungry to receive God's power into your life? Perhaps you've even recited a prayer for this before but weren't really ready yet. However, after learning these truths—how you'll receive power, that this was something even Jesus had to have, that it totally transformed the apostles—you're ready to receive the baptism in the Holy Spirit.

ASK, BELIEVE, AND RECEIVE!

God wants you filled, but you must reach out in faith to take it!

> *For every one that asketh receiveth; and he that seeketh findeth; and to him that knocketh it shall be opened. If a son shall ask bread of any of you that is a father, will he give him a stone? or if he ask a fish, will he for a fish give him a serpent? Or if he shall ask an egg, will he offer him a scorpion? If ye then, being evil, know how to give good gifts unto your children: how much more shall your heavenly Father give the Holy Spirit to them that ask him?*
> LUKE 11:10-13

How much more will your heavenly Father give the Holy Spirit to you! Ask, believe, and receive!

If you're ready, pray out loud the following prayer from your heart:

"Father, I surrender to You completely. I recognize my need for Your power to live the Christian life. Please baptize me in Your Holy Spirit!

"By faith, I receive now the baptism in the Holy Spirit. I take it! It's mine in Jesus's name!

"Father, thank You for giving me the Holy Spirit! Holy Spirit, thank You for coming. You are welcome in my life!"

Continue to praise and thank the Lord for this wonderful gift. Take a few moments to enjoy His presence, and tell Him how much you love Him.

Some people have dramatic experiences receiving the Holy Spirit, and others are genuinely baptized without feeling a thing. One's not better than the other, as long as you received! Don't let outward manifestations, or a lack thereof, enable the devil to talk you out of this gift from God (Matt. 13:19).

If you believed in your heart when you prayed, then God's Word promises that you received. **"Therefore I say unto you, What things soever ye desire, when ye pray, believe that ye receive them, and ye shall have them"** (Mark 11:24). God always honors His Word. Believe it! As you stepped out in faith to obey the direct command of Jesus (John 20:22), you received the baptism in the Holy Spirit.

Congratulations! You've been filled with God's supernatural power! As you learn to tap into this power, your life will never be the same. For the rest of this study guide, I'm going to share about an important way you can draw His power out.

— OUTLINE —

I. God wants you baptized in the Holy Spirit!

   A. His longing to fill, control, and empower you far surpasses your desire to be filled, controlled, and empowered.

   B. In fact, the Holy Spirit has been eagerly waiting for you to open your heart and invite Him in.

   C. Some groups erroneously teach that you must "travail" and wait on God to receive this experience.

   D. This idea is based upon a misinterpretation of Acts 1:4-5, which says,

   > *And, being assembled together with them, commanded them that they should not depart from Jerusalem, but wait for the promise of the Father, which, saith he, ye have heard of me. For John truly baptized with water; but ye shall be baptized with the Holy Ghost not many days hence.*

   E. Jesus commanded the disciples to wait for the baptism because the Holy Spirit had not yet been poured out upon the earth.

   F. Pentecost was God's appointed time to pour out the Holy Spirit (Acts 2:1 and 4).

   G. Since He's already been given, there's no need to wait!

   H. The baptism in the Holy Spirit is a ***gift***, not something you can earn by travail or holiness (Luke 11:13).

   I. If you could rid yourself of all the sin in your life and be perfect before receiving the Holy Spirit, you wouldn't need Him!

II. You need to desire the baptism in the Holy Spirit wholeheartedly.

   A. If you are persuaded and hungry, receiving can be as simple as praying a prayer.

   B. Occasionally, someone needs a period of time to grow in their hunger and desire to receive.

   C. Where are you today?

   D. Are you ready to commit yourself to the Holy Spirit without reservation?

   E. Perhaps you've even recited a prayer for this before but weren't really ready yet.

   F. However, after learning these truths—how you'll receive power, that this was something even Jesus had to have, that it totally transformed the apostles—you're ready to receive the baptism in the Holy Spirit.

III. God wants you filled, but you must reach out in faith to take it!

> *For every one that asketh receiveth; and he that seeketh findeth; and to him that knocketh it shall be opened. If a son shall ask bread of any of you that is a father, will he give him a stone? or if he ask a fish, will he for a fish give him a serpent? Or if he shall ask an egg, will he offer him a scorpion? If ye then, being evil, know how to give good gifts unto your children: how much more shall your heavenly Father give the Holy Spirit to them that ask him?*
>
> LUKE 11:10-13

A. Ask, believe, and receive!

B. If you're ready, pray out loud the following prayer from your heart:

"Father, I surrender to You completely. I recognize my need for Your power to live the Christian life. Please baptize me in Your Holy Spirit!

"By faith, I receive now the baptism in the Holy Spirit. I take it! It's mine in Jesus's name!

"Father, thank You for giving me the Holy Spirit! Holy Spirit, thank You for coming. You are welcome in my life!"

C. Some people have dramatic experiences receiving the Holy Spirit, and others are genuinely baptized without feeling a thing.

D. One's not better than the other, as long as you received!

E. Don't let outward manifestations, or a lack thereof, enable the devil to talk you out of this gift from God (Matt. 13:19).

F. If you believed in your heart when you prayed, then God's Word promises that you received—**"Therefore I say unto you, What things soever ye desire, when ye pray, believe that ye receive them, and ye shall have them"** (Mark 11:24).

G. Congratulations! You've been filled with God's supernatural power!

H. As you learn to tap into this power, your life will never be the same.

TEACHER'S
GUIDE

1. God wants you baptized in the Holy Spirit! His longing to fill, control, and empower you far surpasses your desire to be filled, controlled, and empowered. In fact, the Holy Spirit has been eagerly waiting for you to open your heart and invite Him in. Some groups erroneously teach that you must "travail" and wait on God to receive this experience. This idea is based upon a misinterpretation of Acts 1:4-5, which says,

> *And, being assembled together with them, commanded them that they should not depart from Jerusalem, but wait for the promise of the Father, which, saith he, ye have heard of me. For John truly baptized with water; but ye shall be baptized with the Holy Ghost not many days hence.*

Jesus commanded the disciples to wait for the baptism because the Holy Spirit had not yet been poured out upon the earth. Pentecost was God's appointed time to pour out the Holy Spirit (Acts 2:1 and 4). Since He's already been given, there's no need to wait! The baptism in the Holy Spirit is a gift, not something you can earn by travail or holiness (Luke 11:13). If you could rid yourself of all the sin in your life and be perfect before receiving the Holy Spirit, you wouldn't need Him!

1a. God wants you baptized in the Holy Spirit! His longing to fill, control, and empower you far surpasses what?
Your desire to be filled, controlled, and empowered

1b. True or false: The Holy Spirit has been eagerly waiting for you to open your heart and invite Him in.
True

1c. What do some groups erroneously teach?
A. You can receive the baptism in the Holy Spirit anytime after you are born again
B. Moses was reincarnated as a dog
C. You must "travail" and wait on God to receive the baptism in the Holy Spirit
D. All of the above
E. None of the above
C. You must "travail" and wait on God to receive the baptism in the Holy Spirit

1d. Why did Jesus command the disciples to wait for the baptism?
Because the Holy Spirit had not yet been poured out upon the earth

1e. _____ was God's appointed time to pour out the Holy Spirit (Acts 2:1 and 4).
Pentecost

1f. Is the baptism in the Holy Spirit something you can earn by travail or holiness (Luke 11:13)?
No, it's a gift

1g. You wouldn't need the Holy Spirit if you could do what?
Rid yourself of all the sin in your life and be perfect before receiving Him

2. You need to desire the baptism in the Holy Spirit wholeheartedly. If you are persuaded and hungry, receiving can be as simple as praying a prayer. Occasionally, someone needs a period of time to grow in their hunger and desire to receive. Where are you today? Are you ready to commit yourself to the Holy Spirit without reservation? Perhaps you've even recited a prayer for this before but weren't really ready yet. However, after learning these truths—how you'll receive power, that this was something even Jesus had to have, that it totally transformed the apostles—you're ready to receive the baptism in the Holy Spirit.

    2a. You need to desire the baptism in the Holy Spirit _____.
        Wholeheartedly
    2b. If you are persuaded and hungry, receiving can be as simple as…
        A. Standing on your head
        B. Praying a prayer
        C. Engaging in spiritual warfare
        D. All of the above
        E. None of the above
        B. Praying a prayer
    2c. True or false: Occasionally, someone needs a period of time to grow in their hunger and desire to receive.
        True

3. God wants you filled, but you must reach out in faith to take it!

> *For every one that asketh receiveth; and he that seeketh findeth; and to him that knocketh it shall be opened. If a son shall ask bread of any of you that is a father, will he give him a stone? or if he ask a fish, will he for a fish give him a serpent? Or if he shall ask an egg, will he offer him a scorpion? If ye then, being evil, know how to give good gifts unto your children: how much more shall your heavenly Father give the Holy Spirit to them that ask him?*
>
> LUKE 11:10-13

Ask, believe, and receive! If you're ready, pray out loud the following prayer from your heart:

> *"Father, I surrender to You completely. I recognize my need for Your power to live the Christian life. Please baptize me in Your Holy Spirit!*
>
> *"By faith, I receive now the baptism in the Holy Spirit. I take it! It's mine in Jesus's name!*
>
> *"Father, thank You for giving me the Holy Spirit! Holy Spirit, thank You for coming. You are welcome in my life!"*

Some people have dramatic experiences receiving the Holy Spirit, and others are genuinely baptized without feeling a thing. One's not better than the other, as long as you received! Don't let outward manifestations, or a lack thereof, enable the devil to talk you out of this gift from God (Matt. 13:19). If you believed in your heart when you prayed, then God's Word promises that you received—**"Therefore I say unto you, What things soever ye desire, when ye pray, believe that ye receive them, and ye shall have them"** (Mark 11:24). Congratulations! You've been filled with God's supernatural power! As you learn to tap into this power, your life will never be the same.

3a. Luke 11:10-13 says, **"For every one that asketh _____; and he that seeketh _____; and to him that knocketh it shall be _____. If a son shall ask bread of any of you that is a father, will he give him a stone? or if he ask a fish, will he for a fish give him a serpent? Or if he shall ask an egg, will he offer him a scorpion? If ye then, being evil, know how to give good gifts unto your children: how much more shall your _____ _____ give the Holy Spirit to them that _____ him?"**
"Receiveth" / "findeth" / "opened" / "heavenly Father" / "ask"

3b. Some people have dramatic experiences receiving the Holy Spirit, and others are genuinely baptized without feeling a thing—is one better than the other, as long as you received?
No

3c. What does God's Word promise you in Mark 11:24?
That if you believed in your heart when you prayed, then you received—"Therefore I say unto you, What things soever ye desire, when ye pray, believe that ye receive them, and ye shall have them"

DISCIPLESHIP
── QUESTIONS ──

1. God wants you baptized in the Holy Spirit! His longing to fill, control, and empower you far surpasses what?

    _____
    _____
    _____

2. True or false: The Holy Spirit has been eagerly waiting for you to open your heart and invite Him in.

3. What do some groups erroneously teach?
    A. You can receive the baptism in the Holy Spirit anytime after you are born again
    B. Moses was reincarnated as a dog
    C. You must "travail" and wait on God to receive the baptism in the Holy Spirit
    D. All of the above
    E. None of the above

4. Why did Jesus command the disciples to wait for the baptism?

    _____
    _____
    _____

5. _____ was God's appointed time to pour out the Holy Spirit (Acts 2:1 and 4).

6. Is the baptism in the Holy Spirit something you can earn by travail or holiness (Luke 11:13)?

    _____
    _____
    _____

7. You wouldn't need the Holy Spirit if you could do what?

    _____
    _____
    _____

8. You need to desire the baptism in the Holy Spirit _____.

9 . If you are persuaded and hungry, receiving can be as simple as…
   A. Standing on your head
   B. Praying a prayer
   C. Engaging in spiritual warfare
   D. All of the above
   E. None of the above

10. True or False: Occasionally, someone needs a period of time to grow in their hunger and desire to receive.

11. Luke 11:10-13 says, **"For every one that asketh _____;
   and he that seeketh _____; and to him that knocketh it shall
   be _____. If a son shall ask bread of any of you that is a father,
   will he give him a stone? or if he ask a fish, will he for a fish give him a serpent? Or
   if he shall ask an egg, will he offer him a scorpion? If ye then, being evil, know how to
   give good gifts unto your children: how much more shall your _____
   _____ give the Holy Spirit to them that _____ him?"**

12. Some people have dramatic experiences receiving the Holy Spirit, and others are genuinely baptized without feeling a thing—is one better than the other, as long as you received?

   _____
   _____
   _____

13. What does God's Word promise you in Mark 11:24?

   _____
   _____
   _____

ANSWER
—KEY—

1. Your desire to be filled, controlled, and empowered

2. True

3. C. You must "travail" and wait on God to receive the baptism in the Holy Spirit

4. Because the Holy Spirit had not yet been poured out upon the earth

5. Pentecost

6. No, it's a gift

7. Rid yourself of all the sin in your life and be perfect before receiving Him

8. Wholeheartedly

9. B. Praying a prayer

10. True

11. **"Receiveth" / "findeth" / "opened" / "heavenly Father" / "ask"**

12. No

13. That if you believed in your heart when you prayed, then you received—**"Therefore I say unto you, What things soever ye desire, when ye pray, believe that ye receive them, and ye shall have them"**

—— SCRIPTURES ——

ACTS 1:4-5

And, being assembled together with them, commanded them that they should not depart from Jerusalem, but wait for the promise of the Father, which, saith he, ye have heard of me. [5] For John truly baptized with water; but ye shall be baptized with the Holy Ghost not many days hence.

ACTS 2:1

And when the day of Pentecost was fully come, they were all with one accord in one place.

ACTS 2:4

And they were all filled with the Holy Ghost, and began to speak with other tongues, as the Spirit gave them utterance.

LUKE 11:10-13

For every one that asketh receiveth; and he that seeketh findeth; and to him that knocketh it shall be opened. [11] If a son shall ask bread of any of you that is a father, will he give him a stone? or if he ask a fish, will he for a fish give him a serpent? [12] Or if he shall ask an egg, will he offer him a scorpion? [13] If ye then, being evil, know how to give good gifts unto your children: how much more shall your heavenly Father give the Holy Spirit to them that ask him?

MATTHEW 13:19

When any one heareth the word of the kingdom, and understandeth it not, then cometh the wicked one, and catcheth away that which was sown in his heart. This is he which received seed by the way side.

MARK 11:24

Therefore I say unto you, What things soever ye desire, when ye pray, believe that ye receive them, and ye shall have them.

JOHN 20:22

And when he had said this, he breathed on them, and saith unto them, Receive ye the Holy Ghost.

SPEAKING
IN
TONGUES

God's Word reveals that speaking in tongues is one of the first manifestations to occur when you receive the baptism in the Holy Spirit.

Jesus's disciples spoke in tongues immediately after receiving the Holy Spirit.

> *And when the day of Pentecost was fully come, they were all with one accord in one place. And suddenly there came a sound from heaven as of a rushing mighty wind, and it filled all the house where they were sitting. And there appeared unto them cloven tongues like as of fire, and it sat upon each of them. And they were all filled with the Holy Ghost, and began to speak with other tongues, as the Spirit gave them utterance.*
>
> ACTS 2:1-4

As Peter preached the Gospel to the entire household of Cornelius, they received both salvation and the baptism in the Holy Spirit.

> *While Peter yet spake these words, the Holy Ghost fell on all them which heard the word. And they of the circumcision which believed were astonished, as many as came with Peter, because that on the Gentiles also was poured out the gift of the Holy Ghost. For they heard them speak with tongues, and magnify God.*
>
> ACTS 10:44-46

Speaking in tongues was outward evidence that these brand-new believers had truly received the Holy Spirit.

Peter used this fact to prove to the rest of the Jewish believers (who weren't there in person) that these Gentiles had indeed been born again.

> *And as I began to speak, the Holy Ghost fell on them, as on us at the beginning. Then remembered I the word of the Lord, how that he said, John indeed baptized with water; but ye shall be baptized with the Holy Ghost. Forasmuch then as God gave them the like gift as he did unto us, who believed on the Lord Jesus Christ; what was I, that I could withstand God? When they heard these things, they held their peace, and glorified God, saying, Then hath God also to the Gentiles granted repentance unto life.*
>
> ACTS 11:15-18

Paul ministered the baptism in the Holy Spirit to Apollos' converts in Ephesus. **"And when Paul had laid his hands upon them, the Holy Ghost came on them; and they spake with tongues, and prophesied"** (Acts 19:6). Speaking in tongues comes with the baptism in the Holy Spirit.

EVERY SPIRIT-BAPTIZED BELIEVER

Philip went down to Samaria and evangelized. Many people believed on Jesus when they heard his message and saw the miracles that he did (Acts 8:5-8). Later, Peter and John came to minister the baptism in the Holy Spirit (Acts 8:14-17). As the Samaritans began to receive, one of the new converts, who had been a professional sorcerer, saw them speaking in tongues and selfishly lusted for this power. Peter and John rebuked him for trying to buy God's gift (Acts 8:18-24).

Those who argue against speaking in tongues as initial evidence for the baptism in the Holy Spirit try to use Acts 8 to support their point. However, even though these scriptures don't directly say that the people of Samaria spoke in tongues, there's still plenty of evidence to imply it. Speaking in tongues was present every other time the Holy Spirit was poured out in the book of Acts. Also, this recently converted sorcerer *saw something* when the baptism was ministered, and it caused him to offer the apostles money in exchange for the supernatural ability to impart the Holy Spirit (Acts 8:18). In order to maintain biblical consistency, this visible demonstration of power must have been speaking in tongues.

Speaking in tongues is an immediate audible manifestation of the Holy Spirit available to every Spirit-baptized believer. It's something you can do to help prove that you've received Him. However, tongues won't automatically force their way up out of your mouth just because you've been baptized. The Holy Spirit will never make you do something against your will. Therefore, you must choose to speak in tongues.

DARKNESS TO DAYLIGHT

Personally, I stumbled into the baptism in the Holy Spirit. I had been seeking the Lord with all of my heart and crying out for Him to fill me with His power. On March 23, 1968, He dramatically answered my prayer by baptizing me in the Holy Spirit. At the time, I had no idea what this was, because I'd never been taught about it. All I knew was that my intimate encounter with God had left me supernaturally empowered.

Revelation knowledge immediately began to flow. Before receiving the baptism in the Holy Spirit, I always had to trust what the preacher told me, and I assumed it was true—there wasn't any assurance in my heart or understanding of my own; I just followed their example and did what I was told. Then I received the Holy Spirit, and the One who had written the Bible started explaining it to me. He began revealing things to my heart. Instead of receiving information from the outside in, God Himself was teaching me from the inside out! John 14:26 describes this: **"But the Comforter, which is the Holy Ghost, whom the Father will send in my name, he shall teach you all things, and bring all things to your remembrance, whatsoever I have said unto you."** The difference was daylight and darkness!

In addition to revelation knowledge, I became bold and passionate for the Lord. God's awesome love and glorious presence constantly overwhelmed me. Witnessing to people changed from being a religious chore into a daily delight. The sick received healing when I prayed for them. However, these wonderful things combined to create some problems as well. For instance, my newfound zeal also got me kicked out of my church!

RELIGIOUS PREJUDICE OVERCOME

Everything indicated that I had been baptized in the Holy Spirit, except I didn't speak in tongues. Why? I'd been taught against it! The church I was raised in didn't believe in the baptism in the Holy Spirit and thought that tongues were of the devil. Ignorance and wrong teaching predisposed me against this gift. Although speaking in tongues was available, negative feelings and fear prevented me from using it.

It took me a long time to renew my mind to what God's Word said about my new relationship with the Holy Spirit. Two-and-a-half years after receiving the baptism, I discovered that speaking in tongues was a valid gift from God for today. Then another six months passed before I understood enough to yield to the Holy Spirit and actually speak in tongues. Until I saw what God's Word said about this, my faith wasn't strong enough to walk in it (Rom. 10:17).

If it weren't for my religious prejudice, I could have spoken in tongues as soon as I was baptized in the Holy Spirit. However, those thoughts kept me from enjoying God's gift because their root was unbelief. Until I overcame them and brought myself to the point of voluntarily stepping out in faith, I couldn't speak in tongues. But as soon as I did, my life changed just as dramatically as when I first received the Holy Spirit!

You don't have to speak in tongues—you get to! Besides, there's really no good reason not to. Speaking in tongues releases God's power in your life, and it's available to every Christian who has received the baptism in the Holy Spirit. If you're not speaking in tongues, you're missing out!

— OUTLINE —

I. God's Word reveals that speaking in tongues is one of the first manifestations to occur when you receive the baptism in the Holy Spirit.

  A. Jesus's disciples spoke in tongues immediately after receiving the Holy Spirit.

  And when the day of Pentecost was fully come, they were all with one accord in one place. And suddenly there came a sound from heaven as of a rushing mighty wind, and it filled all the house where they were sitting. And there appeared unto them cloven tongues like as of fire, and it sat upon each of them. And they were all filled with the Holy Ghost, and began to speak with other tongues, as the Spirit gave them utterance.
  ACTS 2:1-4

  B. As Peter preached the Gospel to the entire household of Cornelius, they received both salvation and the baptism in the Holy Spirit.

  While Peter yet spake these words, the Holy Ghost fell on all them which heard the word. And they of the circumcision which believed were astonished, as many as came with Peter, because that on the Gentiles also was poured out the gift of the Holy Ghost. For they heard them speak with tongues, and magnify God.
  ACTS 10:44-46

  C. Speaking in tongues was outward evidence that these brand-new believers had truly received the Holy Spirit.

  D. Peter used this fact to prove to the rest of the Jewish believers (who weren't there in person) that these Gentiles had indeed been born again.

  And as I began to speak, the Holy Ghost fell on them, as on us at the beginning. Then remembered I the word of the Lord, how that he said, John indeed baptized with water; but ye shall be baptized with the Holy Ghost. Forasmuch then as God gave them the like gift as he did unto us, who believed on the Lord Jesus Christ; what was I, that I could withstand God? When they heard these things, they held their peace, and glorified God, saying, Then hath God also to the Gentiles granted repentance unto life.
  ACTS 11:15-18

  E. Paul ministered the baptism in the Holy Spirit to Apollos' converts in Ephesus—**"And when Paul had laid his hands upon them, the Holy Ghost came on them; and they spake with tongues, and prophesied"** (Acts 19:6).

II. Those who argue against speaking in tongues as initial evidence for the baptism in the Holy Spirit try to use Acts 8 to support their point (Acts 8:5-8 and 14-24).

A. However, even though these scriptures don't directly say that the people of Samaria spoke in tongues, there's still plenty of evidence to imply it.

B. Speaking in tongues was present every other time the Holy Spirit was poured out in the book of Acts.

C. Speaking in tongues is an immediate audible manifestation of the Holy Spirit available to every Spirit-baptized believer.

D. It's something you can do to help prove that you've received Him.

E. However, tongues won't automatically force their way up out of your mouth just because you've been baptized.

F. The Holy Spirit will never make you do something against your will; therefore, you must choose to speak in tongues.

III. Personally, I stumbled into the baptism in the Holy Spirit.

A. I had been seeking the Lord with all of my heart and crying out for Him to fill me with His power.

B. On March 23, 1968, He dramatically answered my prayer by baptizing me in the Holy Spirit.

C. At the time, I had no idea what this was, because I'd never been taught about it—all I knew was that my intimate encounter with God had left me supernaturally empowered.

D. Before receiving the baptism in the Holy Spirit, I always had to trust what the preacher told me, and I assumed it was true—there wasn't any assurance in my heart or understanding of my own.

E. Then I received the Holy Spirit, and the One who had written the Bible started explaining it to me.

F. John 14:26 describes this: **"But the Comforter, which is the Holy Ghost, whom the Father will send in my name, he shall teach you all things, and bring all things to your remembrance, whatsoever I have said unto you."**

G. In addition to revelation knowledge, I became bold and passionate for the Lord.

H. God's awesome love and glorious presence constantly overwhelmed me.

I. Witnessing to people changed from being a religious chore into a daily delight.

IV. Everything indicated that I had been baptized in the Holy Spirit, except I didn't speak in tongues.

A. Why? I'd been taught against it!

B. Ignorance and wrong teaching predisposed me against this gift.

C. Although speaking in tongues was available, negative feelings and fear prevented me from using it.

D. It took me a long time to renew my mind to what God's Word said about my new relationship with the Holy Spirit.

E. Until I saw what God's Word said about this, my faith wasn't strong enough to walk in it (Rom. 10:17).

F. If it weren't for my religious prejudice, I could have spoken in tongues as soon as I was baptized in the Holy Spirit.

G. You don't have to speak in tongues—you get to!

H. Besides, there's really no good reason not to.

I. Speaking in tongues releases God's power in your life, and it's available to every Christian who has received the baptism in the Holy Spirit.

J. If you're not speaking in tongues, you're missing out!

TEACHER'S
GUIDE

1. God's Word reveals that speaking in tongues is one of the first manifestations to occur when you receive the baptism in the Holy Spirit. Jesus's disciples spoke in tongues immediately after receiving the Holy Spirit.

> *And when the day of Pentecost was fully come, they were all with one accord in one place. And suddenly there came a sound from heaven as of a rushing mighty wind, and it filled all the house where they were sitting. And there appeared unto them cloven tongues like as of fire, and it sat upon each of them. And they were all filled with the Holy Ghost, and began to speak with other tongues, as the Spirit gave them utterance.*
>
> ACTS 2:1-4

As Peter preached the Gospel to the entire household of Cornelius, they received both salvation and the baptism in the Holy Spirit.

> *While Peter yet spake these words, the Holy Ghost fell on all them which heard the word. And they of the circumcision which believed were astonished, as many as came with Peter, because that on the Gentiles also was poured out the gift of the Holy Ghost. For they heard them speak with tongues, and magnify God.*
>
> ACTS 10:44-46

Speaking in tongues was outward evidence that these brand-new believers had truly received the Holy Spirit. Peter used this fact to prove to the rest of the Jewish believers (who weren't there in person) that these Gentiles had indeed been born again.

> *And as I began to speak, the Holy Ghost fell on them, as on us at the beginning. Then remembered I the word of the Lord, how that he said, John indeed baptized with water; but ye shall be baptized with the Holy Ghost. Forasmuch then as God gave them the like gift as he did unto us, who believed on the Lord Jesus Christ; what was I, that I could withstand God? When they heard these things, they held their peace, and glorified God, saying, Then hath God also to the Gentiles granted repentance unto life.*
>
> ACTS 11:15-18

Paul ministered the baptism in the Holy Spirit to Apollos' converts in Ephesus—**"And when Paul had laid his hands upon them, the Holy Ghost came on them; and they spake with tongues, and prophesied"** (Acts 19:6).

1a. As revealed in God's Word, what is one of the first manifestations of the baptism in the Holy Spirit?
Speaking in tongues

1b. Jesus' disciples spoke in tongues _____ after receiving the Holy Spirit.
   A. A few hours
   B. A few days
   C. A few years
   D. All of the above
   E. None of the above
   E. None of the above

1c. Acts 10:44-46 says, **"While Peter yet spake these words, the Holy Ghost _____ on all them which heard the word. And they of the circumcision which believed were astonished, as many as came with Peter, because that on the Gentiles also was poured out the gift of the Holy Ghost. For they heard them _____ with tongues, and _____ God."**
   "Fell" / "speak" / "magnify"

1d. True or false: Peter used this fact to prove to the rest of the Jewish believers that these Gentiles had indeed been born again (Acts 11:15-18).
   True

2. Those who argue against speaking in tongues as initial evidence for the baptism in the Holy Spirit try to use Acts 8 to support their point (Acts 8:5-8 and 14-24). However, even though these scriptures don't directly say that the people of Samaria spoke in tongues, there's still plenty of evidence to imply it. Speaking in tongues was present every other time the Holy Spirit was poured out in the book of Acts. Speaking in tongues is an immediate audible manifestation of the Holy Spirit available to every Spirit-baptized believer. It's something you can do to help prove that you've received Him. However, tongues won't automatically force their way up out of your mouth just because you've been baptized. The Holy Spirit will never make you do something against your will; therefore, you must choose to speak in tongues.

   2a. What chapter of the Bible do people use to argue against speaking in tongues as initial evidence for the baptism in the Holy Spirit?
      Acts 8
   2b. Why is that chapter used?
      These scriptures don't directly say that the people of Samaria spoke in tongues (although there's still plenty of evidence to imply it)
   2c. Speaking in tongues is an immediate audible manifestation of the Holy Spirit that is what?
      Available to every Spirit-baptized believer
   2d. The Holy Spirit will _____ make you do something against your will; therefore, you must _____ to speak in tongues.
      Never / choose

3. Personally, I stumbled into the baptism in the Holy Spirit. I had been seeking the Lord with all of my heart and crying out for Him to fill me with His power. On March 23, 1968, He dramatically answered my prayer by baptizing me in the Holy Spirit. At the time, I had no idea what this was, because I'd never been taught about it—all I knew was that my intimate encounter with God had left me supernaturally empowered. Before receiving the baptism in the Holy Spirit, I always had to trust what the preacher told me, and I assumed it was true—there wasn't any assurance in my heart or understanding of my own. Then I received the Holy Spirit, and the One who had written the Bible started explaining it to me. John 14:26 describes this: **"But the Comforter, which is the Holy Ghost, whom the Father will send in my name, he shall teach you all things, and bring all things to your remembrance, whatsoever I have said unto you."** In addition to revelation knowledge, I became bold and passionate for the Lord. God's awesome love and glorious presence constantly overwhelmed me. Witnessing to people changed from being a religious chore into a daily delight.

    3a. What two things happened to Andrew after he received the baptism in the Holy Spirit?
        He received revelation knowledge, and he became bold and passionate for the Lord

4. Everything indicated that I had been baptized in the Holy Spirit, except I didn't speak in tongues. Why? I'd been taught against it! Ignorance and wrong teaching predisposed me against this gift. Although speaking in tongues was available, negative feelings and fear prevented me from using it. It took me a long time to renew my mind to what God's Word said about my new relationship with the Holy Spirit. Until I saw what God's Word said about this, my faith wasn't strong enough to walk in it (Rom. 10:17). If it weren't for my religious prejudice, I could have spoken in tongues as soon as I was baptized in the Holy Spirit. You don't have to speak in tongues—you get to! Besides, there's really no good reason not to. Speaking in tongues releases God's power in your life, and it's available to every Christian who has received the baptism in the Holy Spirit. If you're not speaking in tongues, you're missing out!

4a. Did Andrew speak in tongues right away?
      No
4b. What did Andrew have to do then?
      Renew his mind to what God's Word said about his new relationship with the Holy Spirit

DISCIPLESHIP
──QUESTIONS──

1. As revealed in God's Word, what is one of the first manifestations of the baptism in the Holy Spirit?

   _____

   _____

   _____

2. Jesus' disciples spoke in tongues _____ after receiving the Holy Spirit.
   A. A few hours
   B. A few days
   C. A few years
   D. All of the above
   E. None of the above

3. Acts 10:44-46 says, **"While Peter yet spake these words, the Holy Ghost _____ on all them which heard the word. And they of the circumcision which believed were astonished, as many as came with Peter, because that on the Gentiles also was poured out the gift of the Holy Ghost. For they heard them _____ with tongues, and _____ God."**

4. True or false: Peter used this fact to prove to the rest of the Jewish believers that these Gentiles had indeed been born again (Acts 11:15-18).

5. What chapter of the Bible do people use to argue against speaking in tongues as initial evidence for the baptism in the Holy Spirit?

   _____

   _____

   _____

6. Why is that chapter used?

   _____

   _____

   _____

7. Speaking in tongues is an immediate audible manifestation of the Holy Spirit that is what?

   _____

   _____

   _____

8. The Holy Spirit will _____ make you do something against your will; therefore, you must _____ to speak in tongues.

9. What two things happened to Andrew after he received the baptism in the Holy Spirit?
    _____
    _____
    _____

10. Did Andrew speak in tongues right away?
    _____
    _____
    _____

11. What did Andrew have to do then?
    _____
    _____
    _____

ANSWER
—KEY—

1. Speaking in tongues

2. E. None of the above

3. **"Fell" / "speak" / "magnify"**

4. True

5. Acts 8

6. These scriptures don't directly say that the people of Samaria spoke in tongues (although there's still plenty of evidence to imply it)

7. Available to every Spirit-baptized believer

8. Never / choose

9. He received revelation knowledge, and he became bold and passionate for the Lord

10. No

11. Renew his mind to what God's Word said about his new relationship with the Holy Spirit

—— SCRIPTURES ——

ACTS 2:1-4

And when the day of Pentecost was fully come, they were all with one accord in one place. [2] And suddenly there came a sound from heaven as of a rushing mighty wind, and it filled all the house where they were sitting. [3] And there appeared unto them cloven tongues like as of fire, and it sat upon each of them. [4] And they were all filled with the Holy Ghost, and began to speak with other tongues, as the Spirit gave them utterance.

ACTS 10:44-46

While Peter yet spake these words, the Holy Ghost fell on all them which heard the word. [45] And they of the circumcision which believed were astonished, as many as came with Peter, because that on the Gentiles also was poured out the gift of the Holy Ghost. [46] For they heard them speak with tongues, and magnify God. Then answered Peter.

ACTS 11:15-18

And as I began to speak, the Holy Ghost fell on them, as on us at the beginning. [16] Then remembered I the word of the Lord, how that he said, John indeed baptized with water; but ye shall be baptized with the Holy Ghost. [17] Forasmuch then as God gave them the like gift as he did unto us, who believed on the Lord Jesus Christ; what was I, that I could withstand God? [18] When they heard these things, they held their peace, and glorified God, saying, Then hath God also to the Gentiles granted repentance unto life.

ACTS 19:6

And when Paul had laid his hands upon them, the Holy Ghost came on them; and they spake with tongues, and prophesied.

ACTS 8:5-8

Then Philip went down to the city of Samaria, and preached Christ unto them. [6] And the people with one accord gave heed unto those things which Philip spake, hearing and seeing the miracles which he did. [7] For unclean spirits, crying with loud voice, came out of many that were possessed with them: and many taken with palsies, and that were lame, were healed. [8] And there was great joy in that city.

ACTS 8:14-24

Now when the apostles which were at Jerusalem heard that Samaria had received the word of God, they sent unto them Peter and John: [15] Who, when they were come down, prayed for them, that they might receive the Holy Ghost: [16] (For as yet he was fallen upon none of them: only they were baptized in the name of the Lord Jesus.) [17] Then laid they their hands on them, and they received the Holy Ghost. [18] And when Simon saw that through laying on of the apostles' hands the Holy Ghost was given, he offered them money, [19] Saying, Give me also this power, that on whomsoever I lay hands, he may receive the Holy Ghost. [20] But Peter said unto him, Thy money perish with thee, because thou hast thought that the gift of God may be purchased with money. [21] Thou hast neither part nor lot in this matter: for thy heart is not right in the sight of God. [22] Repent therefore of this thy wickedness, and pray God, if perhaps the thought of thine heart may be forgiven thee. [23] For I perceive that thou art in the gall of bitterness, and in the bond of iniquity. [24] Then answered Simon, and said, Pray ye to the Lord for me, that none of these things which ye have spoken come upon me.

JOHN 14:26

But the Comforter, which is the Holy Ghost, whom the Father will send in my name, he shall teach you all things, and bring all things to your remembrance, whatsoever I have said unto you.

ROMANS 10:17

So then faith cometh by hearing, and hearing by the word of God.

PROOF
FOR
TODAY

God's Word clearly teaches that the gift of tongues is for today. This can best be seen in the three chapters of the Bible that deal specifically with the gifts of the Holy Spirit—1 Corinthians 12, 13, and 14. In addition to speaking in tongues, the other gifts are the word of wisdom, the word of knowledge, faith, gifts of healing, working of miracles, prophecy, discerning of spirits, and interpretation of tongues (1 Cor. 12:8-10). (Although an exciting study in itself, further explanation of each individual gift is beyond the scope of our present purpose.)

The local body at Corinth was one of the most carnal churches in the entire New Testament. A man had committed incest with his father's wife (1 Cor. 5:1). Believers were suing each other (1 Cor. 6:1 and 6-7). They divided themselves according to their favorite Bible teacher (1 Cor. 3:3-5). Gluttony and drunkenness characterized the Lord's Supper (1 Cor. 11:20-22). Tongues were being given in church services without interpretation (1 Cor. 14:26-28). Paul rebuked and corrected the Corinthians for all of this immaturity and sin.

These believers were carnal in spite of the gifts of the Spirit—not because of them! It's wrong to assume that the gifts are bad for you just because the Corinthians had so many problems. Actually, the opposite is true! Although maturity isn't instantly granted, the gifts of the Holy Spirit do promote spiritual growth. This is why three different times, Paul advised this carnal, sinful bunch to earnestly **desire spiritual gifts** (1 Cor. 14:1, see also 1 Cor. 12:31 and 14:39). He knew the gifts would help them mature. That's good proof that you should be speaking in tongues.

WHOM DO YOU BELIEVE?

I started talking about the Lord once to a woman whose house I was painting. When she asked me why I'd left the Baptist church, I told her that they kicked me out after I received the baptism in the Holy Spirit.

"Are you talking about speaking in tongues?" she inquired.

"Yes, that's part of it. I do speak in tongues, and that's why they asked me to leave the church."

She thought for a moment and then politely added, "Well, my church would have kicked you out too."

I asked "Why would they do that?" and showed her 1 Corinthians 14:39. "The Bible clearly says here, **'Forbid not to speak with tongues.'**"

I've never forgotten her candid reply: "Well, there are lots of things in the Bible our church doesn't believe."

With that, I knew I couldn't minister to her anymore, because God's Word was not the final authority in her Christian life. She, like so many others, had chosen to believe her denomination's doctrines above God's Word. This is why 1 Corinthians 13 remains the most misunderstood passage of Scripture regarding the gifts of the Holy Spirit today.

BETTER WITH LOVE

The gifts of the Holy Spirit are meant to be operated in love. This explains why Paul wrote **"But covet earnestly the best gifts: and yet shew I unto you a more excellent way"** (1 Cor. 12:31) as he launched into his famous love passage (1 Cor. 13). Some people have tried to say that love is the **"more excellent way."** However, the context clearly shows that all of Paul's comments concerning love in chapter 13 pertain specifically to the use of the gifts of the Holy Spirit that are listed in chapter 12 and expounded on in chapter 14. His point was not that love is better than the gifts but rather that operating the gifts in love is better than using them without it.

The Holy Spirit doesn't control you like a puppet. He leads, guides, and inspires you to speak in tongues and operate the other gifts, but you are the one who actually does it. Therefore, it's possible to operate in the gifts carnally, make mistakes, and fail to be motivated by love.

> *Though I speak with the tongues of men and of angels, and have not charity, I am become as sounding brass, or a tinkling cymbal. And though I have the gift of prophecy, and understand all mysteries, and all knowledge; and though I have all faith, so that I could remove mountains, and have not charity, I am nothing.*
>
> 1 CORINTHIANS 13:1-2

It doesn't matter which gift you're operating in—tongues, prophecy, faith—there's no benefit apart from the right motive. Therefore, let love motivate your use of every gift of the Spirit—including speaking in tongues!

In fact, God's love should be the motivation for everything you do. **"And though I bestow all my goods to feed the poor, and though I give my body to be burned, and have not charity, it profiteth me nothing"** (1 Cor. 13:3). Whether you attend church because you feel you have to or give into an offering out of sheer obligation, apart from love, they profit you nothing. From God's point of view, your motive is more important than your action.

UNTIL THAT WHICH IS PERFECT IS COME

People who reject the baptism in the Holy Spirit twist 1 Corinthians 13:8-10 in order to support their position that tongues passed away with the early church:

Charity never faileth: but whether there be prophecies, they shall fail; whether there be tongues, they shall cease; whether there be knowledge, it shall vanish away. For we know in part, and we prophesy in part. But when that which is perfect is come, then that which is in part shall be done away.
1 CORINTHIANS 13:8-10

They claim that God only gave the gifts of the Holy Spirit (speaking in tongues, prophecy, gifts of healing, working of miracles, etc.) to the early church because the Bible wasn't written yet. Asserting that the Bible is **"that which is perfect,"** they justify their conclusion that God doesn't do these things anymore. Nonsense!

If you read that passage in its context, you can easily see what it's really saying. Remember, Paul's subject for this entire section of Scripture (1 Cor. 12-14) is properly operating in the gifts of the Holy Spirit. He just finished saying that the gifts should be used in love (1 Cor. 13:1-3). First Corinthians 13:4-7 describes what that looks like. Then, in verse 8, the Word states that when tongues cease, knowledge will too. Living in what's been popularly called "The Information Age," you and I both know that this hasn't happened yet. In fact, God's Word prophesies that in the end times, knowledge will greatly increase (Dan. 12:4).

*For we know in part, and we prophesy in part. But **when that which is perfect is come**, then that which is in part shall be done away. When I was a child, I spake as a child, I understood as a child, I thought as a child: but when I became a man, I put away childish things. For now we see through a glass, darkly; but **then** face to face: now I know in part; but **then** shall I know even as also I am known.*
1 CORINTHIANS 13:9-12, UNDERLINE MINE

The **"then"** in verse 12 refers to **"when that which is perfect is come."** At the time **"when that which is perfect is come,"** you will see Jesus face to face. Since that won't happen until the Lord's Second Coming or you die and go to be with Him, neither has tongues passed away yet.

"That which is perfect" refers to your glorified body, not the Bible. Yes, the Bible is perfect—inspired, inerrant, infallible—but it's not what this phrase is pointing to. When you receive your glorified body, you will no longer see through a glass darkly or know in part. In your glorified body, you will see Jesus face to face and know Him even as He knows you— completely. For now, speaking in tongues has been given to help you grow in the knowledge of Him. In your glorified body, you won't need tongues or the other gifts of the Holy Spirit— prophecy, the word of wisdom, discerning of spirits, interpretation of tongues, etc.—to reveal the Lord anymore, because you'll already know Him fully.

The very scriptures people use to dismiss the gifts of the Holy Spirit actually prove their validity for today! As long as your knowledge of Him is incomplete, the gifts of the Spirit will function. Until you see Jesus face to face in your glorified body, you need to be speaking in tongues. Since **"that which is perfect"** has yet to come, God's miraculous power continues on earth today just as it did for the early church. You would have to already be corrupted with a predisposed, religious mindset in order to honestly look at these scriptures and interpret them as saying "God's miraculous power has passed away." **"Brethren, covet to prophesy, and forbid not to speak with tongues"** (1 Cor. 14:39)!

MIRACULOUS PROOF

Why do some people fight so hard against the truth that the baptism of the Holy Spirit and His miraculous power are for today? Two main reasons are wrong teaching and a rejection of personal responsibility. Doctrines of men can render the Word of God ineffective. That's what happens when you hold on to religious tradition instead of God's Word (Mark 7:13). Also, there's a fear of having to produce biblical results. If you profess to believe in the baptism in the Holy Spirit, speaking in tongues, casting out demons, healing, and miracles, then that puts pressure on you to manifest them (Mark 16:17-18). Most people don't want to accept this kind of personal responsibility.

Instead, many hide behind a convenient theology. Calling themselves "Christian," they quickly confess that their sins are forgiven, while their lives offer very little proof. It's easy to profess "My sins are forgiven" because you can't see a sin, and you can't see when it's forgiven. However, if miracles are really part of the Christian life, then there are things you can do to prove their reality. For instance, you can speak in tongues, cast a demon out, see blind eyes and deaf ears open, or even raise someone from the dead (I have personally done all of these things on multiple occasions and know many others who have done them as well—to God be the glory). In order to sit in front of the television, living carnal, self-centered lives while defending their position of being forgiven, some so-called "Christians" choose to believe only what God's Word says about forgiveness of sins while conveniently ignoring the rest. They may or may not truly be saved. Who would know?

Jesus used miracles to prove salvation.

> *Whether is it easier to say to the sick of the palsy, Thy sins be forgiven thee; or to say, Arise, and take up thy bed, and walk? But that ye may know that the Son of man hath power on earth to forgive sins, (he saith to the sick of the palsy,) I say unto thee, Arise, and take up thy bed, and go thy way into thine house.*
>
> MARK 2:9-11

Confronted by unbelieving religious leaders, Jesus asked them which would be harder to say, "Your sins are forgiven" or "Take up your bed and walk." No one can see a sin forgiven, but everyone in that crowded room, including the Pharisees, would be able to see if this man was healed or not. Either he would get up and walk, or Jesus's words would be totally violated. Therefore, "Take up your bed and walk" was definitely harder to say!

The people knew that if Jesus could perform that which was hardest, surely He could do the least. **"And immediately he arose, took up the bed, and went forth before them all; insomuch that they were all amazed, and glorified God"** (Mark 2:12). Jesus used the fact that He could heal bodies and perform miracles in the physical realm to substantiate the fact that He could also do things, like forgiving sins, in the spiritual realm.

The reason many people hide behind this false doctrine that miracles passed away is so they can claim to be in relationship with God without ever doing anything to demonstrate it. That's just a convenient theology! The truth is that God still does miracles today, and you should be speaking in tongues until you receive your glorified body!

— OUTLINE —

I. God's Word clearly teaches that the gift of tongues is for today.

   A. This can best be seen in the three chapters of the Bible that deal specifically with the gifts of the Holy Spirit—1 Corinthians 12, 13, and 14.

   B. The local body at Corinth was one of the most carnal churches in the entire New Testament.

   C. These believers were carnal in spite of the gifts of the Spirit—not because of them!

   D. It's wrong to assume that the gifts are bad for you just because the Corinthians had so many problems.

   E. Although maturity isn't instantly granted, the gifts of the Holy Spirit do promote spiritual growth.

   F. This is why three different times, Paul advised this carnal, sinful bunch to earnestly **"desire spiritual gifts"** (1 Cor. 14:1, see also 1 Cor. 12:31 and 14:39).

II. I started talking about the Lord once to a woman whose house I was painting.

   A. When she asked me why I'd left the Baptist church, I told her that they kicked me out after I received the baptism in the Holy Spirit. "Are you talking about speaking in tongues?" she inquired. I answered, "Yes, that's part of it. I do speak in tongues, and that's why they asked me to leave the church." She said, "Well, my church would have kicked you out too." I showed her 1 Corinthians 14:39 and said, "The Bible clearly says here, **'Forbid not to speak with tongues.'"** I've never forgotten her candid reply: "Well, there are lots of things in the Bible our church doesn't believe."

   B. With that, I knew I couldn't minister to her anymore, because God's Word was not the final authority in her Christian life.

   C. She, like so many others, had chosen to believe her denomination's doctrines above God's Word.

   D. This is why 1 Corinthians 13 remains the most misunderstood passage of Scripture regarding the gifts of the Holy Spirit today.

III. The gifts of the Holy Spirit are meant to be operated in love.

   A. This explains why Paul wrote **"But covet earnestly the best gifts: and yet shew I unto you a more excellent way"** (1 Cor. 12:31) as he launched into his famous love passage (1 Cor. 13).

B. Some people have tried to say that love is the **"more excellent way"**; however, the context clearly shows that all of Paul's comments concerning love in chapter 13 pertain specifically to the use of the gifts of the Holy Spirit that are listed in chapter 12 and expounded on in chapter 14.

C. His point was not that love is better than the gifts but rather that operating the gifts in love is better than using them without it.

D. The Holy Spirit doesn't control you like a puppet—He leads, guides, and inspires you to speak in tongues and operate the other gifts, but you are the one who actually does it.

E. Therefore, it's possible to operate in the gifts carnally, make mistakes, and fail to be motivated by love.

Though I speak with the tongues of men and of angels, and have not charity, I am become as sounding brass, or a tinkling cymbal. And though I have the gift of prophecy, and understand all mysteries, and all knowledge; and though I have all faith, so that I could remove mountains, and have not charity, I am nothing.

1 CORINTHIANS 13:1-2

F. It doesn't matter which gift you're operating in—tongues, prophecy, faith—there's no benefit apart from the right motive.

G. In fact, God's love should be the motivation for everything you do—**"And though I bestow all my goods to feed the poor, and though I give my body to be burned, and have not charity, it profiteth me nothing"** (1 Cor. 13:3).

H. From God's point of view, your motive is more important than your action.

IV. People who reject the baptism in the Holy Spirit twist 1 Corinthians 13:8-10 in order to support their position that tongues passed away with the early church:

Charity never faileth: but whether there be prophecies, they shall fail; whether there be tongues, they shall cease; whether there be knowledge, it shall vanish away. For we know in part, and we prophesy in part. But when that which is perfect is come, then that which is in part shall be done away.

1 CORINTHIANS 13:8-10

A. They claim that God only gave the gifts of the Holy Spirit (speaking in tongues, prophecy, gifts of healing, working of miracles, etc.) to the early church because the Bible wasn't written yet.

B. Asserting that the Bible is **"that which is perfect,"** they justify their conclusion that God doesn't do these things anymore—nonsense!

C. If you read that passage in its context, you can easily see what it's really saying.

*For we know in part, and we prophesy in part. But **when that which is
perfect is come**, then that which is in part shall be done away. When I was
a child, I spake as a child, I understood as a child, I thought as a child: but
when I became a man, I put away childish things. For now we see through a
glass, darkly; but **then** face to face: now I know in part; but **then** shall I know
even as also I am known.*

1 CORINTHIANS 13:9-12, UNDERLINE MINE

D. The **"then"** in verse 12 refers to **"when that which is perfect is come."**

E. **"That which is perfect"** refers to your glorified body, not the Bible.

F. For now, speaking in tongues has been given to help you grow in the knowledge of Him.

G. In your glorified body, you won't need tongues or the other gifts of the Holy Spirit—prophecy, the word of wisdom, discerning of spirits, interpretation of tongues, etc.—to reveal the Lord anymore, because you'll already know Him fully.

H. The very scriptures people use to dismiss the gifts of the Holy Spirit actually prove their validity for today!

I. As long as your knowledge of Him is incomplete, the gifts of the Spirit will function.

J. Since **"that which is perfect"** has yet to come, God's miraculous power continues on earth today just as it did for the early church.

K. **"Brethren, covet to prophesy, and forbid not to speak with tongues"** (1 Cor. 14:39)!

V. Some people fight so hard against the truth that the baptism of the Holy Spirit and His miraculous power are for today—two main reasons for this are wrong teaching and a rejection of personal responsibility.

A. Doctrines of men can render the Word of God ineffective—that's what happens when you hold on to religious tradition instead of God's Word (Mark 7:13).

B. Also, there's a fear of having to produce biblical results.

C. If you profess to believe in the baptism in the Holy Spirit, speaking in tongues, casting out demons, healing, and miracles, then that puts pressure on you to manifest them (Mark 16:17-18).

D. Instead, many hide behind a convenient theology—calling themselves "Christian," they quickly confess that their sins are forgiven, while their lives offer very little proof.

E. It's easy to profess "My sins are forgiven" because you can't see a sin, and you can't see when it's forgiven.

F. However, if miracles are really part of the Christian life, then there are things you can do to prove their reality.

G. Jesus used miracles to prove salvation.

> *Whether is it easier to say to the sick of the palsy, Thy sins be forgiven thee; or to say, Arise, and take up thy bed, and walk? But that ye may know that the Son of man hath power on earth to forgive sins, (he saith to the sick of the palsy,) I say unto thee, Arise, and take up thy bed, and go thy way into thine house.*
>
> MARK 2:9-11

H. No one can see a sin forgiven, but everyone in that crowded room, including the Pharisees, would be able to see if this man was healed or not.

I. **"And immediately he arose, took up the bed, and went forth before them all; insomuch that they were all amazed, and glorified God"** (Mark 2:12)—Jesus used the fact that He could heal bodies and perform miracles in the physical realm to substantiate the fact that He could also do things, like forgiving sins, in the spiritual realm.

J. The reason many people hide behind this false doctrine that miracles passed away is so they can claim to be in relationship with God without ever doing anything to demonstrate it.

K. The truth is that God still does miracles today, and you should be speaking in tongues until you receive your glorified body!

TEACHER'S
GUIDE

1. God's Word clearly teaches that the gift of tongues is for today. This can best be seen in the three chapters of the Bible that deal specifically with the gifts of the Holy Spirit—1 Corinthians 12, 13, and 14. The local body at Corinth was one of the most carnal churches in the entire New Testament. These believers were carnal in spite of the gifts of the Spirit—not because of them! It's wrong to assume that the gifts are bad for you just because the Corinthians had so many problems. Although maturity isn't instantly granted, the gifts of the Holy Spirit do promote spiritual growth. This is why three different times, Paul advised this carnal, sinful bunch to earnestly **"desire spiritual gifts"** (1 Cor. 14:1, see also 1 Cor. 12:31 and 14:39).

    1a. What are the three chapters in the Bible that best show that the gift of tongues is for today?
        1 Corinthians 12, 13, and 14
    1b. True or false: The Corinthian believers were carnal because of the gifts of the Spirit.
        False
    1c. Although maturity isn't _____ granted, the gifts of the Holy Spirit do _____ spiritual growth.
        Instantly / promote

2. I started talking about the Lord once to a woman whose house I was painting. When she asked me why I'd left the Baptist church, I told her that they kicked me out after I received the baptism in the Holy Spirit. "Are you talking about speaking in tongues?" she inquired. I answered, "Yes, that's part of it. I do speak in tongues, and that's why they asked me to leave the church." She said, "Well, my church would have kicked you out too." I showed her 1 Corinthians 14:39 and said, "The Bible clearly says here, **'Forbid not to speak with tongues.'"** I've never forgotten her candid reply: "Well, there are lots of things in the Bible our church doesn't believe." With that, I knew I couldn't minister to her anymore, because God's Word was not the final authority in her Christian life. She, like so many others, had chosen to believe her denomination's doctrines above God's Word. This is why 1 Corinthians 13 remains the most misunderstood passage of Scripture regarding the gifts of the Holy Spirit today.

    2a. What scripture did Andrew use in dealing with the woman whose house he was painting?
        1 Corinthians 14:39
    2b. What makes 1 Corinthians 13 one of the most misunderstood passages of Scripture regarding the gifts of the Holy Spirit?
        People have not made the Word of God the final authority in their Christian lives and they have chosen to believe their denomination's doctrines above God's Word

3. The gifts of the Holy Spirit are meant to be operated in love. This explains why Paul wrote **"But covet earnestly the best gifts: and yet shew I unto you a more excellent way"** (1 Cor. 12:31) as he launched into his famous love passage (1 Cor. 13). Some people have tried to say that love is the **"more excellent way"**; however, the context clearly shows that all of Paul's comments concerning love in chapter 13 pertain specifically to the use of the gifts of the Holy Spirit that are listed in chapter 12 and expounded on in chapter 14. His point was not that love is better than the gifts but rather that operating the gifts in love is better than using them without it. The Holy Spirit doesn't control you like a puppet—He leads, guides, and inspires you to speak in tongues and operate the other gifts, but you are the one who actually does it. Therefore, it's possible to operate in the gifts carnally, make mistakes, and fail to be motivated by love.

> *Though I speak with the tongues of men and of angels, and have not charity, I am become as sounding brass, or a tinkling cymbal. And though I have the gift of prophecy, and understand all mysteries, and all knowledge; and though I have all faith, so that I could remove mountains, and have not charity, I am nothing.*
>
> 1 CORINTHIANS 13:1-2

It doesn't matter which gift you're operating in—tongues, prophecy, faith—there's no benefit apart from the right motive. In fact, God's love should be the motivation for everything you do—**"And though I bestow all my goods to feed the poor, and though I give my body to be burned, and have not charity, it profiteth me nothing"** (1 Cor. 13:3). From God's point of view, your motive is more important than your action.

 3a. The gifts of the Holy Spirit are meant to be operated...
  A. In a hospital
  B. Carnally
  C. In love
  D. All of the above
  E. None of the above
  C. In love
 3b. Paul preceded his famous love passage (1 Cor. 13) with 1 Corinthians 12:31, which says, **"But covet earnestly the best gifts: and yet shew I unto you a _____."**
  "More excellent way"
 3c. What was Paul's point regarding 1 Corinthians 12:31 and 1 Corinthians 13?
  That operating the gifts in love is better than using them without it, not that love is better than the gifts
 3d. True or false: The Holy Spirit doesn't control you like a puppet—He leads, guides, and inspires you to speak in tongues and operate the other gifts, but you are the one who actually does it.
  True
 3e. Is there any benefit to operating in the gifts apart from the right motive?
  No
 3f. What should be your motivation for everything you do?
  God's love

4. People who reject the baptism in the Holy Spirit twist 1 Corinthians 13:8-10 in order to support their position that tongues passed away with the early church:

> *Charity never faileth: but whether there be prophecies, they shall fail; whether there be tongues, they shall cease; whether there be knowledge, it shall vanish away. For we know in part, and we prophesy in part. But when that which is perfect is come, then that which is in part shall be done away.*
>
> 1 CORINTHIANS 13:8-10

They claim that God only gave the gifts of the Holy Spirit (speaking in tongues, prophecy, gifts of healing, working of miracles, etc.) to the early church because the Bible wasn't written yet. Asserting that the Bible is **"that which is perfect,"** they justify their conclusion that God doesn't do these things anymore—nonsense! If you read that passage in its context, you can easily see what it's really saying.

> *For we know in part, and we prophesy in part. But **when that which is perfect is come**, then that which is in part shall be done away. When I was a child, I spake as a child, I understood as a child, I thought as a child: but when I became a man, I put away childish things. For now we see through a glass, darkly; but **then** face to face: now I know in part; but **then** shall I know even as also I am known.*
>
> 1 CORINTHIANS 13:9-12, UNDERLINE MINE

The **"then"** in verse 12 refers to **"when that which is perfect is come." "That which is perfect"** refers to your glorified body, not the Bible. For now, speaking in tongues has been given to help you grow in the knowledge of Him. In your glorified body, you won't need tongues or the other gifts of the Holy Spirit—prophecy, the word of wisdom, discerning of spirits, interpretation of tongues, etc.—to reveal the Lord anymore, because you'll already know Him fully. The very scriptures people use to dismiss the gifts of the Holy Spirit actually prove their validity for today! As long as your knowledge of Him is incomplete, the gifts of the Spirit will function. Since **"that which is perfect"** has yet to come, God's miraculous power continues on earth today just as it did for the early church. **"Brethren, covet to prophesy, and forbid not to speak with tongues"** (1 Cor. 14:39)!

   4a. What do people who reject the baptism in the Holy Spirit claim?
   That God only gave the gifts of the Holy Spirit (speaking in tongues, prophecy, gifts of healing, working of miracles, etc.) to the early church because the Bible wasn't written yet

   4b. First Corinthians 13:9-12 says, **"For we know in part, and we prophesy in part. But when that which is _____ is come, then that which is in part shall be done away. When I was a child, I spake as a child, I understood as a child, I thought as a child: but when I became a man, I put away childish things. For now we see through a glass, darkly; but then _____ to _____: now I know in part; but _____ shall I know even as also I am known."**
   "Perfect" / "face" / "face" / "then"

   4c. What does "that which is perfect" refer to and what does it not refer to?
   It refers to your glorified body and not to the Bible

   4d. Why has speaking in tongues been given, for now?
   To help your grow in the knowledge of Him

   4e. Will you need the gifts of the Holy Spirit once you receive your glorified body? Why or why not?
   No, because you'll already know Him fully

5. Some people fight so hard against the truth that the baptism of the Holy Spirit and His miraculous power are for today—two main reasons for this are wrong teaching and a rejection of personal responsibility. Doctrines of men can render the Word of God ineffective—that's what happens when you hold on to religious tradition instead of God's Word (Mark 7:13). Also, there's a fear of having to produce biblical results. If you profess to believe in the baptism in the Holy Spirit, speaking in tongues, casting out demons, healing, and miracles, then that puts pressure on you to manifest them (Mark 16:17-18). Instead, many hide behind a convenient theology—calling themselves "Christian," they quickly confess that their sins are forgiven, while their lives offer very little proof. It's easy to profess "My sins are forgiven" because you can't see a sin, and you can't see when it's forgiven. However, if miracles are really part of the Christian life, then there are things you can do to prove their reality. Jesus used miracles to prove salvation.

> *Whether is it easier to say to the sick of the palsy, Thy sins be forgiven thee; or to say, Arise, and take up thy bed, and walk? But that ye may know that the Son of man hath power on earth to forgive sins, (he saith to the sick of the palsy,) I say unto thee, Arise, and take up thy bed, and go thy way into thine house.*
>
> MARK 2:9-11

No one can see a sin forgiven, but everyone in that crowded room, including the Pharisees, would be able to see if this man was healed or not. **"And immediately he arose, took up the bed, and went forth before them all; insomuch that they were all amazed, and glorified God"** (Mark 2:12)—Jesus used the fact that He could heal bodies and perform miracles in the physical realm to substantiate the fact that He could also do things, like forgiving sins, in the spiritual realm. The reason many people hide behind this false doctrine that miracles passed away is so they can claim to be in relationship with God without ever doing anything to demonstrate it. The truth is that God still does miracles today, and you should be speaking in tongues until you receive your glorified body!

5a. What are the two main reasons some people fight so hard against the truth that the baptism of the Holy Spirit and His miraculous power are for today?
   A. Wrong teaching and a lack of knowledge
   B. Wrong teaching and a rejection of personal responsibility
   C. A crowd mentality and a rejection of personal responsibility
   D. All of the above
   E. None of the above
   B. Wrong teaching and a rejection of personal responsibility

5b. True or false: It's hard to profess "My sins are forgiven" because you can't see a sin, and you can't see when it's forgiven.
   False

5c. True or false: If miracles are really part of the Christian life, then there is nothing you can do to prove their reality.
   False

5d. **"Whether is it _____ to say to the sick of the palsy, Thy sins be forgiven thee; or to say, Arise, and take up thy bed, and walk? But that ye may know that the Son of man hath power on earth to _____ sins, (he saith to the sick of the palsy,) I say unto thee, Arise, and take up thy bed, and go thy way into thine house"** (Mark 2:9-11).
<u>**"Easier" / "forgive"**</u>

5e. Did Jesus use the fact that He could heal bodies and perform miracles in the physical realm to substantiate the fact that He could also do things, like forgiving sins, in the spiritual realm?
<u>**Yes**</u>

DISCIPLESHIP
── QUESTIONS ──

1. What are the three chapters in the Bible that best show that the gift of tongues is for today?

   _____

   _____

   _____

2. True or false: The Corinthian believers were carnal because of the gifts of the Spirit.

3. Although maturity isn't _____ granted, the gifts of the Holy Spirit do _____ spiritual growth.

4. What scripture did Andrew use in dealing with the woman whose house he was painting?

   _____

   _____

   _____

5. What makes 1 Corinthians 13 one of the most misunderstood passages of Scripture regarding the gifts of the Holy Spirit?

   _____

   _____

   _____

6. The gifts of the Holy Spirit are meant to be operated...
   A. In a hospital
   B. Carnally
   C. In love
   D. All of the above
   E. None of the above

7. Paul preceded his famous love passage (1 Cor. 13) with 1 Corinthians 12:31, which says, **"But covet earnestly the best gifts: and yet shew I unto you a**

   _____ _____ _____**."**

8. What was Paul's point regarding 1 Corinthians 12:31 and 1 Corinthians 13?

   _____

   _____

   _____

9. True or false: The Holy Spirit doesn't control you like a puppet—He leads, guides, and inspires you to speak in tongues and operate the other gifts, but you are the one who actually does it.

10. Is there any benefit to operating in the gifts apart from the right motive?

    _____
    _____
    _____

11. What should be your motivation for everything you do?

    _____
    _____
    _____

12. What do people who reject the baptism in the Holy Spirit claim?

    _____
    _____
    _____

13. First Corinthians 13:9-12 says, **"For we know in part, and we prophesy in part. But when that which is _____ is come, then that which is in part shall be done away. When I was a child, I spake as a child, I understood as a child, I thought as a child: but when I became a man, I put away childish things. For now we see through a glass, darkly; but then _____ to _____: now I know in part; but _____ shall I know even as also I am known."**

14. What does **"that which is perfect"** refer to and what does it not refer to?

    _____
    _____
    _____

15. Why has speaking in tongues been given, for now?

    _____
    _____
    _____

16. Will you need the gifts of the Holy Spirit once you receive your glorified body? Why or why not?

    _____
    _____
    _____

17. What are the two main reasons some people fight so hard against the truth that the baptism of the Holy Spirit and His miraculous power are for today?
    A. Wrong teaching and a lack of knowledge
    B. Wrong teaching and a rejection of personal responsibility
    C. A crowd mentality and a rejection of personal responsibility
    D. All of the above
    E. None of the above

18. True or false: It's hard to profess "My sins are forgiven" because you can't see a sin, and you can't see when it's forgiven.

19. True or false: If miracles are really part of the Christian life, then there is nothing you can do to prove their reality.

20. **"Whether is it _____ to say to the sick of the palsy, Thy sins be forgiven thee; or to say, Arise, and take up thy bed, and walk? But that ye may know that the Son of man hath power on earth to _____ sins, (he saith to the sick of the palsy,) I say unto thee, Arise, and take up thy bed, and go thy way into thine house"** (Mark 2:9-11).

21. Did Jesus use the fact that He could heal bodies and perform miracles in the physical realm to substantiate the fact that He could also do things, like forgiving sins, in the spiritual realm?
    _____
    _____
    _____

ANSWER
—KEY—

1. 1 Corinthians 12, 13, and 14

2. False

3. Instantly / promote

4. 1 Corinthians 14:39

5. People have not made the Word of God the final authority in their Christian lives and they have chosen to believe their denomination's doctrines above God's Word

6. C. In love

7. **"More excellent way"**

8. That operating the gifts in love is better than using them without it, not that love is better than the gifts

9. True

10. No

11. God's love

12. That God only gave the gifts of the Holy Spirit (speaking in tongues, prophecy, gifts of healing, working of miracles, etc.) to the early church because the Bible wasn't written yet

13. **"Perfect" / "face" / "face" / "then"**

14. It refers to your glorified body and not to the Bible

15. To help your grow in the knowledge of Him

16. No, because you'll already know Him fully

17. B. Wrong teaching and a rejection of personal responsibility

18. False

19. False

20. **"Easier" / "forgive"**

21. Yes

—— SCRIPTURES ——

1 CORINTHIANS 12:8-10

For to one is given by the Spirit the word of wisdom; to another the word of knowledge by the same Spirit; [9] To another faith by the same Spirit; to another the gifts of healing by the same Spirit; [10] To another the working of miracles; to another prophecy; to another discerning of spirits; to another divers kinds of tongues; to another the interpretation of tongues.

1 CORINTHIANS 5:1

It is reported commonly that there is fornication among you, and such fornication as is not so much as named among the Gentiles, that one should have his father's wife.

1 CORINTHIANS 6:1

Dare any of you, having a matter against another, go to law before the unjust, and not before the saints?

1 CORINTHIANS 6:6-7

But brother goeth to law with brother, and that before the unbelievers. [7] Now therefore there is utterly a fault among you, because ye go to law one with another. Why do ye not rather take wrong? why do ye not rather suffer yourselves to be defrauded?

1 CORINTHIANS 3:3-5

For ye are yet carnal: for whereas there is among you envying, and strife, and divisions, are ye not carnal, and walk as men? [4] For while one saith, I am of Paul; and another, I am of Apollos; are ye not carnal? [5] Who then is Paul, and who is Apollos, but ministers by whom ye believed, even as the Lord gave to every man?

1 CORINTHIANS 11:20-22

When ye come together therefore into one place, this is not to eat the Lord's supper. [21] For in eating every one taketh before other his own supper: and one is hungry, and another is drunken. [22] What? have ye not houses to eat and to drink in? or despise ye the church of God, and shame them that have not? What shall I say to you? shall I praise you in this? I praise you not.

1 CORINTHIANS 14:26-28

How is it then, brethren? when ye come together, every one of you hath a psalm, hath a doctrine, hath a tongue, hath a revelation, hath an interpretation. Let all things be done unto edifying. [27] If any man speak in an unknown tongue, let it be by two, or at the most by three, and that by course; and let one interpret. [28] But if there be no interpreter, let him keep silence in the church; and let him speak to himself, and to God.

1 CORINTHIANS 14:1

Follow after charity, and desire spiritual gifts, but rather that ye may prophesy.

1 CORINTHIANS 12:31

But covet earnestly the best gifts: and yet shew I unto you a more excellent way.

1 CORINTHIANS 14:39

Wherefore, brethren, covet to prophesy, and forbid not to speak with tongues.

1 CORINTHIANS 13:1-12

Though I speak with the tongues of men and of angels, and have not charity, I am become as sounding brass, or a tinkling cymbal. [2] And though I have the gift of prophecy, and understand all mysteries, and all knowledge; and though I have all faith, so that I could remove mountains, and have not charity, I am nothing. [3] And though I bestow all my goods to feed the poor, and though I give my body to be burned, and have not charity, it profiteth me nothing. [4] Charity suffereth long, and is kind; charity envieth not; charity vaunteth not itself, is not puffed up, [5] Doth not behave itself unseemly, seeketh not her own, is not easily provoked, thinketh no evil; [6] Rejoiceth not in iniquity, but rejoiceth in the truth; [7] Beareth all things, believeth all things, hopeth all things, endureth all things. [8] Charity never faileth: but whether there be prophecies, they shall fail; whether there be tongues, they shall cease; whether there be knowledge, it shall vanish away. [9] For we know in part, and we prophesy in part. [10] But when that which is perfect is come, then that which is in part shall be done away. [11] When I was a child, I spake as a child, I understood as a child, I thought as a child: but when I became a man, I put away childish things. [12] For now we see through a glass, darkly; but then face to face: now I know in part; but then shall I know even as also I am known.

DANIEL 12:4

But thou, O Daniel, shut up the words, and seal the book, even to the time of the end: many shall run to and fro, and knowledge shall be increased.

MARK 7:13

Making the word of God of none effect through your tradition, which ye have delivered: and many such like things do ye.

MARK 16:17-18

And these signs shall follow them that believe; In my name shall they cast out devils; they shall speak with new tongues; [18] They shall take up serpents; and if they drink any deadly thing, it shall not hurt them; they shall lay hands on the sick, and they shall recover.

MARK 2:9-12

Whether is it easier to say to the sick of the palsy, Thy sins be forgiven thee; or to say, Arise, and take up thy bed, and walk? [10] But that ye may know that the Son of man hath power on earth to forgive sins, (he saith to the sick of the palsy,) [11] I say unto thee, Arise, and take up thy bed, and go thy way into thine house. [12] And immediately he arose, took up the bed, and went forth before them all; insomuch that they were all amazed, and glorified God, saying, We never saw it on this fashion.

BUILD YOURSELF UP

The primary purpose of speaking in tongues is to promote personal spiritual growth.

For he that speaketh in an unknown tongue speaketh not unto men, but unto God: for no man understandeth him; howbeit in the spirit he speaketh mysteries. . . . He that speaketh in an unknown tongue edifieth himself.
1 CORINTHIANS 14:2 AND 4

When you speak in tongues, you're building yourself up spiritually.

You also keep yourself in the love of God. **"But ye, beloved, building up yourselves on your most holy faith, praying in the Holy Ghost, Keep yourselves in the love of God, looking for the mercy of our Lord Jesus Christ unto eternal life"** (Jude 20-21). God's love for you never changes, but your experience of it does. Speaking in tongues helps you fulfill your responsibility to keep yourself aware of and enjoying God's unfailing love.

Speaking in tongues produces rest and spiritual refreshment. **"For with stammering lips and another tongue will he speak to this people. To whom he said, This is the rest wherewith ye may cause the weary to rest; and this is the refreshing"** (Is. 28:11-12). Your spirit is the part of you where God lives. It's brand new, pure, righteous, and holy. When you pray in tongues, you release into your soul and body the rest and refreshment that's already in your spirit.

Personally, I encourage myself by speaking in tongues. Whenever I feel tired or discouraged, I pray in the spirit until rest and refreshment come. Despite negative circumstances and emotions, I'll exercise my faith to pray in tongues until I'm aware of and enjoying God's love again.

Once you realize you can pray in the spirit anytime you choose, you have no excuse to ever be depressed again!

PRAYING PERFECTLY

When you pray in tongues, your natural mind doesn't understand. **"For if I pray in an unknown tongue, my spirit prayeth, but my understanding is unfruitful"** (1 Cor. 14:14). Unless there's an interpretation, your intellect doesn't know what your spirit is praying.

Your spirit has the mind of Christ.

For who hath known the mind of the Lord, that he may instruct him? But we have the mind of Christ.
1 CORINTHIANS 2:16

Your spirit knows all things.

But ye have an unction from the Holy One, and ye know all things.
1 JOHN 2:20

And have put on the new man, which is renewed in knowledge after the
image of him that created him.

COLOSSIANS 3:10

Therefore, your spirit always knows how to pray perfectly for situations, yourself, and others.

There's a big difference between praying from your spirit and praying from your mind. Your natural mind typically has incomplete information. It lacks full knowledge of God's Word, the situation, and the people involved. Therefore, you cannot pray from your intellect with completeness and 100 percent accuracy. However, since your born-again spirit knows all things, it's impossible to pray in tongues without praying God's perfect will!

At times, the Holy Spirit may intercede for someone else through you as you pray in tongues.

Likewise the Spirit also helpeth our infirmities: for we know not what we
should pray for as we ought: but the Spirit itself maketh intercession for us
with groanings which cannot be uttered. And he that searcheth the hearts
knoweth what is the mind of the Spirit, because he maketh intercession for the
saints according to the will of God.

ROMANS 8:26-27

This is especially helpful when your mind is not sure how to pray for a specific person or situation.

As you speak in tongues, you are speaking the hidden wisdom of God. Paul received the revelation for the messages he preached through speaking in tongues.

Howbeit we speak wisdom among them that are perfect: yet not the wisdom
of this world, nor of the princes of this world, that come to nought: But we
speak the wisdom of God in a mystery, even the hidden wisdom, which God
ordained before the world unto our glory.

1 CORINTHIANS 2:6-7

For he that speaketh in an unknown tongue speaketh not unto men,
but unto God: for no man understandeth him; howbeit in the spirit he
speaketh mysteries.

1 CORINTHIANS 14:2

As Paul spoke God's mysteries in tongues, he built himself up spiritually and revelation knowledge came. As you pray in tongues, you'll be built up spiritually as revelation knowledge comes to you too!

— OUTLINE —

I. The primary purpose of speaking in tongues is to promote personal spiritual growth.

> *For he that speaketh in an unknown tongue speaketh not unto men, but unto God: for no man understandeth him; howbeit in the spirit he speaketh mysteries. . . . He that speaketh in an unknown tongue edifieth himself.*
> 1 CORINTHIANS 14:2 AND 4

A. When you speak in tongues, you're building yourself up spiritually.

B. You also keep yourself in the love of God—**"But ye, beloved, building up yourselves on your most holy faith, praying in the Holy Ghost, Keep yourselves in the love of God, looking for the mercy of our Lord Jesus Christ unto eternal life"** (Jude 20-21).

C. Speaking in tongues produces rest and spiritual refreshment—**"For with stammering lips and another tongue will he speak to this people. To whom he said, This is the rest wherewith ye may cause the weary to rest; and this is the refreshing"** (Is. 28:11-12).

D. Your spirit is the part of you where God lives—it's brand new, pure, righteous, and holy.

E. When you pray in tongues, you release into your soul and body the rest and refreshment that's already in your spirit.

F. Once you realize you can pray in the spirit anytime you choose, you have no excuse to ever be depressed again!

II. When you pray in tongues, your natural mind doesn't understand—**"For if I pray in an unknown tongue, my spirit prayeth, but my understanding is unfruitful"** (1 Cor. 14:14).

A. Unless there's an interpretation, your intellect doesn't know what your spirit is praying.

B. Your spirit has the mind of Christ.

> *For who hath known the mind of the Lord, that he may instruct him? But we have the mind of Christ.*
> 1 CORINTHIANS 2:16

C. Your spirit knows all things.

> *But ye have an unction from the Holy One, and ye know all things.*
> 1 JOHN 2:20

> *And have put on the new man, which is renewed in knowledge after the image of him that created him.*
> COLOSSIANS 3:10

D. Therefore, your spirit always knows how to pray perfectly for situations, yourself, and others.

E. There's a big difference between praying from your spirit and praying from your mind.

  i. Your natural mind typically has incomplete information.

  ii. It lacks full knowledge of God's Word, the situation, and the people involved.

  iii. Therefore, you cannot pray from your intellect with completeness and 100 percent accuracy.

F. However, since your born-again spirit knows all things, it's impossible to pray in tongues without praying God's perfect will!

G. At times, the Holy Spirit may intercede for someone else through you as you pray in tongues.

> *Likewise the Spirit also helpeth our infirmities: for we know not what we should pray for as we ought: but the Spirit itself maketh intercession for us with groanings which cannot be uttered. And he that searcheth the hearts knoweth what is the mind of the Spirit, because he maketh intercession for the saints according to the will of God.*
>
> ROMANS 8:26-27

H. As you speak in tongues, you are speaking the hidden wisdom of God.

I. Paul received the revelation for the messages he preached through speaking in tongues.

> *Howbeit we speak wisdom among them that are perfect: yet not the wisdom of this world, nor of the princes of this world, that come to nought: But we speak the wisdom of God in a mystery, even the hidden wisdom, which God ordained before the world unto our glory.*
>
> 1 CORINTHIANS 2:6-7

> *For he that speaketh in an unknown tongue speaketh not unto men, but unto God: for no man understandeth him; howbeit in the spirit he speaketh mysteries.*
>
> 1 CORINTHIANS 14:2

J. As Paul spoke God's mysteries in tongues, he built himself up spiritually and revelation knowledge came—as you pray in tongues, you'll be built up spiritually as revelation knowledge comes to you too!

TEACHER'S
GUIDE

1. The primary purpose of speaking in tongues is to promote personal spiritual growth.

> *For he that speaketh in an unknown tongue speaketh not unto men, but unto God: for no man understandeth him; howbeit in the spirit he speaketh mysteries. . . . He that speaketh in an unknown tongue edifieth himself.*
> 1 CORINTHIANS 14:2 AND 4

When you speak in tongues, you're building yourself up spiritually. You also keep yourself in the love of God—**"But ye, beloved, building up yourselves on your most holy faith, praying in the Holy Ghost, Keep yourselves in the love of God, looking for the mercy of our Lord Jesus Christ unto eternal life"** (Jude 20-21). Speaking in tongues produces rest and spiritual refreshment—**"For with stammering lips and another tongue will he speak to this people. To whom he said, This is the rest wherewith ye may cause the weary to rest; and this is the refreshing"** (Is. 28:11-12). Your spirit is the part of you where God lives—it's brand new, pure, righteous, and holy. When you pray in tongues, you release into your soul and body the rest and refreshment that's already in your spirit. Once you realize you can pray in the spirit anytime you choose, you have no excuse to ever be depressed again!

    1a. What is the primary purpose of speaking in tongues?
        A. To promote personal spiritual growth
        B. So that God can understand you
        C. For the edification of the body of Christ
        D. All of the above
        E. None of the above
        A. To promote personal spiritual growth
    1b. When you speak in tongues, you also keep yourself in the what?
        Love of God
    1c. Isaiah 28:11-12 says, **"For with stammering lips and another** _____ **will he speak to this people. To whom he said, This is the** _____ **wherewith ye may cause the weary to rest; and this is the** _____**."**
        "Tongue" / "rest" / "refreshing"
    1d. When you pray in tongues, you release into your soul and body the rest and refreshment that's where?
        Already in your spirit

2. When you pray in tongues, your natural mind doesn't understand—**"For if I pray in an unknown tongue, my spirit prayeth, but my understanding is unfruitful"** (1 Cor. 14:14). Unless there's an interpretation, your intellect doesn't know what your spirit is praying. Your spirit has the mind of Christ.

> *For who hath known the mind of the Lord, that he may instruct him? But we have the mind of Christ.*
>
> 1 CORINTHIANS 2:16

Your spirit knows all things.

> *But ye have an unction from the Holy One, and ye know all things.*
>
> 1 JOHN 2:20

> *And have put on the new man, which is renewed in knowledge after the image of him that created him.*
>
> COLOSSIANS 3:10

Therefore, your spirit always knows how to pray perfectly for situations, yourself, and others. There's a big difference between praying from your spirit and praying from your mind. Your natural mind typically has incomplete information. It lacks full knowledge of God's Word, the situation, and the people involved. Therefore, you cannot pray from your intellect with completeness and 100 percent accuracy. However, since your born-again spirit knows all things, it's impossible to pray in tongues without praying God's perfect will! At times, the Holy Spirit may intercede for someone else through you as you pray in tongues.

> *Likewise the Spirit also helpeth our infirmities: for we know not what we should pray for as we ought: but the Spirit itself maketh intercession for us with groanings which cannot be uttered. And he that searcheth the hearts knoweth what is the mind of the Spirit, because he maketh intercession for the saints according to the will of God.*
>
> ROMANS 8:26-27

As you speak in tongues, you are speaking the hidden wisdom of God. Paul received the revelation for the messages he preached through speaking in tongues.

> *Howbeit we speak wisdom among them that are perfect: yet not the wisdom of this world, nor of the princes of this world, that come to nought: But we speak the wisdom of God in a mystery, even the hidden wisdom, which God ordained before the world unto our glory.*
>
> 1 CORINTHIANS 2:6-7

> *For he that speaketh in an unknown tongue speaketh not unto men, but unto God: for no man understandeth him; howbeit in the spirit he speaketh mysteries.*
>
> 1 CORINTHIANS 14:2

As Paul spoke God's mysteries in tongues, he built himself up spiritually and revelation knowledge came—as you pray in tongues, you'll be built up spiritually as revelation knowledge comes to you too!

   2a. True or false: Your natural mind understands it when you pray in tongues.
      False
   2b. What is a characteristic of your spirit?
      A. Your spirit has the mind of Christ
      B. Your spirit knows how to pray perfectly for situations, yourself, and others
      C. Your spirit knows all things
      D. All of the above
      E. None of the above
      D. All of the above
   2c. Is there a big difference between praying from your spirit and praying from your mind?
      Yes
   2d. Since your born-again spirit knows all things, it's impossible to do what?
      Pray in tongues without praying God's perfect will
   2e. What passage of Scripture tells you that the Holy Spirit may intercede for someone else through you as you pray in tongues?
      Romans 8:26-27
   2f. As you speak in tongues, you are speaking the _____
_____ _____.

      Hidden wisdom of God

DISCIPLESHIP
── QUESTIONS ──

1. What is the primary purpose of speaking in tongues?
   A. To promote personal spiritual growth
   B. So that God can understand you
   C. For the edification of the body of Christ
   D. All of the above
   E. None of the above

2. When you speak in tongues, you also keep yourself in the what?
   _____
   _____
   _____

3. Isaiah 28:11-12 says, **"For with stammering lips and another** _____
   will he speak to this people. To whom he said, This is the _____
   wherewith ye may cause the weary to rest; and this is the _____**."**

4. When you pray in tongues, you release into your soul and body the rest and refreshment
   that's where?
   _____
   _____
   _____

5. True or false: Your natural mind understands it when you pray in tongues.

6. What is a characteristic of your spirit?
   A. Your spirit has the mind of Christ
   B. Your spirit knows how to pray perfectly for situations, yourself, and others
   C. Your spirit knows all things
   D. All of the above
   E. None of the above

7. Is there a big difference between praying from your spirit and praying from your mind?
   _____
   _____
   _____

8. Since your born-again spirit knows all things, it's impossible to do what?
   _____
   _____
   _____

9. What passage of Scripture tells you that the Holy Spirit may intercede for someone else through you as you pray in tongues?

_____

_____

_____

10. As you speak in tongues, you are speaking the _____

_____ _____ _____ .

ANSWER
—KEY—

1. A. To promote personal spiritual growth

2. Love of God

3. **"Tongue" / "rest" / "refreshing"**

4. Already in your spirit

5. False

6. D. All of the above

7. Yes

8. Pray in tongues without praying God's perfect will

9. Romans 8:26-27

10. Hidden wisdom of God

—— SCRIPTURES ——

1 CORINTHIANS 14:2

For he that speaketh in an unknown tongue speaketh not unto men, but unto God: for no man understandeth him; howbeit in the spirit he speaketh mysteries.

1 CORINTHIANS 14:4

He that speaketh in an unknown tongue edifieth himself; but he that prophesieth edifieth the church.

JUDE 20-21

But ye, beloved, building up yourselves on your most holy faith, praying in the Holy Ghost, [21] Keep yourselves in the love of God, looking for the mercy of our Lord Jesus Christ unto eternal life.

ISAIAH 28:11-12

For with stammering lips and another tongue will he speak to this people. [12] To whom he said, This is the rest wherewith ye may cause the weary to rest; and this is the refreshing: yet they would not hear.

1 CORINTHIANS 14:14

For if I pray in an unknown tongue, my spirit prayeth, but my understanding is unfruitful.

1 CORINTHIANS 2:16

For who hath known the mind of the Lord, that he may instruct him? But we have the mind of Christ.

1 JOHN 2:20

But ye have an unction from the Holy One, and ye know all things.

COLOSSIANS 3:10

And have put on the new man, which is renewed in knowledge after the image of him that created him.

ROMANS 8:26-27

Likewise the Spirit also helpeth our infirmities: for we know not what we should pray for as we ought: but the Spirit itself maketh intercession for us with groanings which cannot be uttered. [27] And he that searcheth the hearts knoweth what is the mind of the Spirit, because he maketh intercession for the saints according to the will of God.

1 CORINTHIANS 2:6-7

Howbeit we speak wisdom among them that are perfect: yet not the wisdom of this world, nor of the princes of this world, that come to nought: [7] But we speak the wisdom of God in a mystery, even the hidden wisdom, which God ordained before the world unto our glory.

INTERPRETATION

When you speak in tongues, you should believe God for the interpretation. ***"Wherefore let him that speaketh in an unknown tongue pray that he may interpret"*** (1 Cor. 14:13). It's beyond your carnal ability to grasp the mysteries and hidden wisdom of God that you're praying in the spirit. However, if you ask Him, God will supernaturally give you the interpretation.

The public use of the gift of tongues in a church service requires interpretation.

> *If any man speak in an unknown tongue, let it be by two, or at the most by three, and that by course; and let one interpret. But if there be no interpreter, let him keep silence in the church; and let him speak to himself, and to God.*
> 1 CORINTHIANS 14:27-28

Without interpretation of a publicly given tongue, some people will think you're crazy:

> *If therefore the whole church be come together into one place, and all speak with tongues, and there come in those that are unlearned, or unbelievers, will they not say that ye are mad?*
> 1 CORINTHIANS 14:23

Certain members of the body are given the vocation of interpretation for public purposes.

> *Now ye are the body of Christ, and members in particular. And God hath set some in the church, first apostles, secondarily prophets, thirdly teachers, after that miracles, then gifts of healings, helps, governments, diversities of tongues. Are all apostles? are all prophets? are all teachers? are all workers of miracles? Have all the gifts of healing? do all speak with tongues? do all interpret?*
> 1 CORINTHIANS 12:27-30

Some people have misunderstood 1 Corinthians 12:29-30 to mean that not everyone should speak in tongues. However, Mark 16:17-18 states:

> *And these signs shall follow them that believe; In my name shall they cast out devils; they shall speak with new tongues; They shall take up serpents; and if they drink any deadly thing, it shall not hurt them; they shall lay hands on the sick, and they shall recover.*

Therefore, some have vocations of speaking and/or interpreting tongues given publicly in a church service, but every Spirit-baptized believer can pray in tongues for personal edification.

OF MEN AND ANGELS

Tongues come in two different types—tongues of men and tongues of angels: **"Though I speak with the tongues of men and of angels"** (1 Cor. 13:1).

Tongues of men are languages that either have been or are spoken on earth. When the disciples were first baptized in the Holy Spirit on Pentecost, they spoke in tongues of men (Acts 2:4-12). This wasn't merely a supernatural acceleration of language learning, because the speakers themselves had no idea what they were saying. The disciples didn't study all those different languages in the room while waiting for the promise! The Holy Spirit suddenly baptized them, and their tongues became a supernatural sign to the unbelievers within earshot whose native languages the disciples were speaking (1 Cor. 14:22).

Tongues of angels are heavenly languages. Every Spirit-baptized believer can pray in the tongues of angels. When you speak mysteries and the hidden wisdom of God, you are speaking in an angelic tongue.

It doesn't matter if you speak in a tongue of men or an angelic tongue—you can ask God for the interpretation!

LIGHT IN MY CLOSET

Learning to believe God for interpretation turned my life around! When I first prayed in tongues after being baptized in the Holy Spirit, I remember hearing God speak to me in my heart as revelation knowledge began to flow. However, when I started sharing what God had shown me in His Word, people criticized and informed me I was wrong because they had never heard these truths before. Feeling isolated and alone, I really struggled with what others were telling me and what I was hearing in my heart. In the midst of all this, I just kept seeking the Lord.

For six months, I meditated on God's Word all day long. As I wrote out hundreds of scriptures daily, I'd focus my attention on each individual word and phrase. After meditating this way for eight to ten hours, God's Word exploded with meaning in my heart, but my mind struggled to understand. So, I'd shut myself in my closet to pray in the spirit for another hour or two. Sitting there underneath my clothes, I'd ask God to interpret to my natural understanding what I'd been studying. Then I'd pray in tongues for the purpose of personal edification.

At the end of that season, my trickle of revelation knowledge suddenly burst forth into a mighty rushing river! In fact, I received so much so fast that I finally told God I couldn't handle any more. It was just more than I could retain! Much of what I'm teaching today—decades later—came as a result of what I learned at that time. I simply prayed in tongues and believed to interpret.

GAIN UNDERSTANDING

All you need to interpret tongues for personal edification is to gain understanding. When you're praying by yourself, you don't have to stop and get an interpretation in English. This method—praying out loud in tongues, then waiting until the English interpretation is given—works well in public, but it's not the only way to receive interpretation. You just need your mind to become fruitful.

God encouraged me through an experience that happened while I was still quite new at this. Since I'd been taught against tongues so strongly, I still wrestled with doubts about whether all my praying in the spirit was really beneficial or not. After spending two hours speaking in tongues one morning, someone whom I hadn't seen in four years showed up at my house. He knocked on the door, rushed in without greeting me, plopped down on my couch, and burst into tears. My first thought was, *I should have been praying in English instead of wasting all morning praying in tongues!* Then it dawned on me, *How would I have known to pray for this guy unless I had been praying in tongues?* My spirit had been praying perfectly!

All of a sudden, faith rose up inside as I stopped him mid-sentence, interrupting his blubbering attempt to explain the situation. By revelation knowledge, I finished describing the rest of his problem—and nailed it! This supernatural demonstration of God's power and love totally set him free! Through this, the Lord confirmed to me that I'd been praying in tongues for this situation earlier, and all I had to do was interpret. What I spoke to this man was the interpretation!

MIND YOUR HEAD!

When you pray in tongues, your mind can be occupied with something else. Since your spirit's praying and not your brain, your mind can wander. You can even think about things totally unrelated to God. That's why some people like to read the Word, enjoy godly music, or listen to Bible teaching while they pray in tongues. Others pray in the spirit while working, driving, or doing household chores. Personally, I've trained myself to pray with my understanding while praying in tongues.

When I'd pray in the spirit over longer periods of time, people whom I hadn't thought of in years would come to mind. At first, I just dismissed it, but when they'd suddenly call, send a letter, or even show up at my house—like that fellow did—I began realizing that God was giving me interpretations. They weren't always word for word but also came as impressions, pictures, and unctions. As I recognized the Lord bringing these people to mind, I'd start praying for them. Then I'd follow through and see miracles happen every time!

God led me to call a good friend of mine one time after praying in tongues. We'd been out of touch with each other for several years. He answered the phone and immediately hung up on me. His reaction seemed strange, since I knew God had prompted me to call. While sitting at my desk pondering this, the phone rang. Sure enough, it was my friend! He explained that he had just told God how he had spent his entire life ministering to others, but now that he was in need, nobody was ministering to him. My friend had barely finished praying "God, please send somebody to encourage me, or I'm going to quit the ministry!" when the phone rang and there I was. He was so startled, he hung up the receiver! This whole incident resulted from interpreting a tongue.

You can do this while praying for people, when you need wisdom for a challenging situation, or simply to understand a particular scripture. Just take the person, situation, or passage, and begin praying in tongues over it. As you're praying, ask the Lord to show you what it means. Although understanding may not always come at that exact moment, God will give you an interpretation.

My friend prays in tongues over church services he's going to minister in. He prefers to receive the interpretation right away so he'll know in advance what God wants to do, who's going to be healed of what, etc. Personally, I don't always like to receive the interpretation right away. If God supernaturally told me what was going to happen at a church service a week away, my mind would try to analyze the situation and figure it all out in the meantime. I pray in tongues often without receiving anything from the Lord at that moment. However, when I need it a week or a month later, I'll ask God for the interpretation of what I've been praying in tongues. At that point, I receive exactly what I need from the Holy Spirit.

As you step out in faith to pray in tongues and believe God for the interpretation, you'll receive exactly what you need from the Holy Spirit too!

—— OUTLINE ——

I. When you speak in tongues, you should believe God for the interpretation—**"Wherefore let him that speaketh in an unknown tongue pray that he may interpret"** (1 Cor. 14:13).

    A. It's beyond your carnal ability to grasp the mysteries and hidden wisdom of God that you're praying in the spirit.

    B. However, if you ask Him, God will supernaturally give you the interpretation.

    C. The public use of the gift of tongues in a church service requires interpretation.

> *If any man speak in an unknown tongue, let it be by two, or at the most by three, and that by course; and let one interpret. But if there be no interpreter, let him keep silence in the church; and let him speak to himself, and to God.*
> 1 CORINTHIANS 14:27-28

    D. Without interpretation of a publicly given tongue, some people will think you're crazy:

> *If therefore the whole church be come together into one place, and all speak with tongues, and there come in those that are unlearned, or unbelievers, will they not say that ye are mad?*
> 1 CORINTHIANS 14:23

    E. Certain members of the body are given the vocation of interpretation for public purposes.

> *Now ye are the body of Christ, and members in particular. And God hath set some in the church, first apostles, secondarily prophets, thirdly teachers, after that miracles, then gifts of healings, helps, governments, diversities of tongues. Are all apostles? are all prophets? are all teachers? are all workers of miracles? Have all the gifts of healing? do all speak with tongues? do all interpret?*
> 1 CORINTHIANS 12:27-30

    F. Some people have misunderstood 1 Corinthians 12:29-30 to mean that not everyone should speak in tongues.

    G. However, Mark 16:17-18 states:

> *And these signs shall follow them that believe; In my name shall they cast out devils; they shall speak with new tongues; They shall take up serpents; and if they drink any deadly thing, it shall not hurt them; they shall lay hands on the sick, and they shall recover.*

    H. Therefore, some have vocations of speaking and/or interpreting tongues given publicly in a church service, but every Spirit-baptized believer can pray in tongues for personal edification.

II. Tongues come in two different types—tongues of men and tongues of angels: **"Though I speak with the tongues of men and of angels"** (1 Cor. 13:1).

   A. Tongues of men are languages that either have been or are spoken on earth.

   B. When the disciples were first baptized in the Holy Spirit on Pentecost, they spoke in tongues of men (Acts 2:4-12).

      i. This wasn't merely a supernatural acceleration of language learning, because the speakers themselves had no idea what they were saying.

      ii. The Holy Spirit suddenly baptized them, and their tongues became a supernatural sign to the unbelievers within earshot whose native languages the disciples were speaking (1 Cor. 14:22).

   C. Tongues of angels are heavenly languages.

      i. Every Spirit-baptized believer can pray in the tongues of angels.

      ii. When you speak mysteries and the hidden wisdom of God, you are speaking in an angelic tongue.

   D. It doesn't matter if you speak in a tongue of men or an angelic tongue—you can ask God for the interpretation!

III. All you need to interpret tongues for personal edification is to gain understanding.

   A. When you're praying by yourself, you don't have to stop and get an interpretation in English.

   B. This method—praying out loud in tongues, then waiting until the English interpretation is given—works well in public, but it's not the only way to receive interpretation.

   C. You just need your mind to become fruitful.

IV. When you pray in tongues, your mind can be occupied with something else.

   A. Since your spirit's praying and not your brain, your mind can wander—you can even think about things totally unrelated to God.

   B. Personally, I've trained myself to pray with my understanding while praying in tongues.

   C. You can do this while praying for people, when you need wisdom for a challenging situation, or simply to understand a particular scripture—just take the person, situation, or passage, and begin praying in tongues over it.

   D. As you're praying, ask the Lord to show you what it means.

   E. Although understanding may not always come at that exact moment, God will give you an interpretation.

F.   As you step out in faith to pray in tongues and believe God for the interpretation, you'll receive exactly what you need from the Holy Spirit!

TEACHER'S
GUIDE

1. When you speak in tongues, you should believe God for the interpretation—**"Wherefore let him that speaketh in an unknown tongue pray that he may interpret"** (1 Cor. 14:13). It's beyond your carnal ability to grasp the mysteries and hidden wisdom of God that you're praying in the spirit. However, if you ask Him, God will supernaturally give you the interpretation. The public use of the gift of tongues in a church service requires interpretation.

> *If any man speak in an unknown tongue, let it be by two, or at the most by three, and that by course; and let one interpret. But if there be no interpreter, let him keep silence in the church; and let him speak to himself, and to God.*
> 1 CORINTHIANS 14:27-28

Without interpretation of a publicly given tongue, some people will think you're crazy:

> *If therefore the whole church be come together into one place, and all speak with tongues, and there come in those that are unlearned, or unbelievers, will they not say that ye are mad?*
> 1 CORINTHIANS 14:23

Certain members of the body are given the vocation of interpretation for public purposes.

> *Now ye are the body of Christ, and members in particular. And God hath set some in the church, first apostles, secondarily prophets, thirdly teachers, after that miracles, then gifts of healings, helps, governments, diversities of tongues. Are all apostles? are all prophets? are all teachers? are all workers of miracles? Have all the gifts of healing? do all speak with tongues? do all interpret?*
> 1 CORINTHIANS 12:27-30

Some people have misunderstood 1 Corinthians 12:29-30 to mean that not everyone should speak in tongues. However, Mark 16:17-18 states:

> *And these signs shall follow them that believe; In my name shall they cast out devils; they shall speak with new tongues; They shall take up serpents; and if they drink any deadly thing, it shall not hurt them; they shall lay hands on the sick, and they shall recover.*

Therefore, some have vocations of speaking and/or interpreting tongues given publicly in a church service, but every Spirit-baptized believer can pray in tongues for personal edification.

1a. **"Wherefore let him that speaketh in an unknown tongue pray that he may _____"** (1 Cor. 14:13).
   "Interpret"
1b. True or false: It's within your carnal ability to grasp the mysteries and hidden wisdom of God that you're praying in the spirit.
   False

1c. God will supernaturally give you the interpretation if you what?
Ask Him

1d. What have some people done with 1 Corinthians 12:29-30?
They have misunderstood it to mean that not everyone should speak in tongues

1e. Some have vocations of speaking and/or interpreting tongues given
_____ in a church service, but _____ Spirit-
baptized believer can pray in tongues for personal edification.
Publicly / every

2. Tongues come in two different types—tongues of men and tongues of angels: **"Though I speak with the tongues of men and of angels"** (1 Cor. 13:1). Tongues of men are languages that either have been or are spoken on earth. When the disciples were first baptized in the Holy Spirit on Pentecost, they spoke in tongues of men (Acts 2:4-12). This wasn't merely a supernatural acceleration of language learning, because the speakers themselves had no idea what they were saying. The Holy Spirit suddenly baptized them, and their tongues became a supernatural sign to the unbelievers within earshot whose native languages the disciples were speaking (1 Cor. 14:22). Tongues of angels are heavenly languages. Every Spirit-baptized believer can pray in the tongues of angels. When you speak mysteries and the hidden wisdom of God, you are speaking in an angelic tongue. It doesn't matter if you speak in a tongue of men or an angelic tongue—you can ask God for the interpretation!

2a. Tongues come in two different types (1 Cor. 13:1). What are they?
   A. Tongues of Farsi and of Tamil
   B. Tongues of men and of angels
   C. Tongues of old and of new
   D. All of the above
   E. None of the above
   B. Tongues of men and of angels

2b. What are tongues of men?
Languages that either have been or are spoken on earth

2c. What are tongues of angels?
Heavenly languages

3. All you need to interpret tongues for personal edification is to gain understanding. When you're praying by yourself, you don't have to stop and get an interpretation in English. This method—praying out loud in tongues, then waiting until the English interpretation is given—works well in public, but it's not the only way to receive interpretation. You just need your mind to become fruitful.

3a. When you're praying by yourself, do you need to stop and get an interpretation in English?
No

3b. Do you just need your mind to become fruitful?
Yes

4. When you pray in tongues, your mind can be occupied with something else. Since your spirit's praying and not your brain, your mind can wander—you can even think about things totally unrelated to God. Personally, I've trained myself to pray with my understanding while praying in tongues. You can do this while praying for people, when you need wisdom for a challenging situation, or simply to understand a particular scripture—just take the person, situation, or passage, and begin praying in tongues over it. As you're praying, ask the Lord to show you what it means. Although understanding may not always come at that exact moment, God will give you an interpretation. As you step out in faith to pray in tongues and believe God for the interpretation, you'll receive exactly what you need from the Holy Spirit!

    4a. True or false: When you pray in tongues, your mind can be occupied with something else.
       True
    4b. Since your spirit's praying and not your brain, what can happen?
       Your mind can wander—you can even think about things totally unrelated to God
    4c. You can pray with your understanding while praying for _____, when you need _____ for a challenging situation, or simply to _____ a particular scripture.
       People / wisdom / understand
    4d. What should you do as you're praying?
       Ask the Lord to show you what it means
    4e. Although understanding may not always come _____ _____ _____, God will give you an interpretation.
       A. At that exact moment
       B. On the full moon
       C. With prayer and fasting
       D. All of the above
       E. None of the above
       A. At that exact moment
    4f. As you step out in faith to pray in tongues and believe God for the interpretation, what will happen?
       You'll receive exactly what you need from the Holy Spirit

DISCIPLESHIP
── QUESTIONS ──

1. **"Wherefore let him that speaketh in an unknown tongue pray that he may**
   _____" (1 Cor. 14:13).

2. True or false: It's within your carnal ability to grasp the mysteries and hidden wisdom of God that you're praying in the spirit.

3. God will supernaturally give you the interpretation if you what?
   _____
   _____
   _____

4. What have some people done with 1 Corinthians 12:29-30?
   _____
   _____
   _____

5. Some have vocations of speaking and/or interpreting tongues given _____ in a church service, but _____ Spirit-baptized believer can pray in tongues for personal edification.

6. Tongues come in two different types (1 Cor. 13:1). What are they?
   A. Tongues of Farsi and of Tamil
   B. Tongues of men and of angels
   C. Tongues of old and of new
   D. All of the above
   E. None of the above

7. What are tongues of men?
   _____
   _____
   _____

8. What are tongues of angels?
   _____
   _____
   _____

9. When you're praying by yourself, do you need to stop and get an interpretation in English?

    _____

    _____

    _____

10. Do you just need your mind to become fruitful?

    _____

    _____

    _____

11. True or false: When you pray in tongues, your mind can be occupied with something else.

12. Since your spirit's praying and not your brain, what can happen?

    _____

    _____

    _____

13. You can pray with your understanding while praying for _____,
    when you need _____ for a challenging situation, or simply to
    _____ a particular scripture.

14. What should you do as you're praying?

    _____

    _____

    _____

15. Although understanding may not always come _____
    _____ _____ _____, God will
    give you an interpretation.
    A. At that exact moment
    B. On the full moon
    C. With prayer and fasting
    D. All of the above
    E. None of the above

16. As you step out in faith to pray in tongues and believe God for the interpretation, what
    will happen?

    _____

    _____

    _____

ANSWER
—KEY—

1. **"Interpret"**

2. False

3. Ask Him

4. They have misunderstood it to mean that not everyone should speak in tongues

5. Publicly / every

6. B. Tongues of men and of angels

7. Languages that either have been or are spoken on earth

8. Heavenly languages

9. No

10. Yes

11. True

12. Your mind can wander—you can even think about things totally unrelated to God

13. People / wisdom / understand

14. Ask the Lord to show you what it means

15. A. At that exact moment

16. You'll receive exactly what you need from the Holy Spirit

— SCRIPTURES —

1 CORINTHIANS 14:13

Wherefore let him that speaketh in an unknown tongue pray that he may interpret.

1 CORINTHIANS 14:27-28

If any man speak in an unknown tongue, let it be by two, or at the most by three, and that by course; and let one interpret. [28] But if there be no interpreter, let him keep silence in the church; and let him speak to himself, and to God.

1 CORINTHIANS 14:22-23

Wherefore tongues are for a sign, not to them that believe, but to them that believe not: but prophesying serveth not for them that believe not, but for them which believe. [23] If therefore the whole church be come together into one place, and all speak with tongues, and there come in those that are unlearned, or unbelievers, will they not say that ye are mad?

1 CORINTHIANS 12:27-30

Now ye are the body of Christ, and members in particular. [28] And God hath set some in the church, first apostles, secondarily prophets, thirdly teachers, after that miracles, then gifts of healings, helps, governments, diversities of tongues. [29] Are all apostles? are all prophets? are all teachers? are all workers of miracles? [30] Have all the gifts of healing? do all speak with tongues? do all interpret?

MARK 16:17-18

And these signs shall follow them that believe; In my name shall they cast out devils; they shall speak with new tongues; [18] They shall take up serpents; and if they drink any deadly thing, it shall not hurt them; they shall lay hands on the sick, and they shall recover.

1 CORINTHIANS 13:1

Though I speak with the tongues of men and of angels, and have not charity, I am become as sounding brass, or a tinkling cymbal.

ACTS 2:4-12

And they were all filled with the Holy Ghost, and began to speak with other tongues, as the Spirit gave them utterance. [5] And there were dwelling at Jerusalem Jews, devout men, out of every nation under heaven. [6] Now when this was noised abroad, the multitude came together, and were confounded, because that every man heard them speak in his own language. [7] And they were all amazed and marvelled, saying one to another, Behold, are not all these which speak Galilaeans? [8] And how hear we every man in our own tongue, wherein we were born? [9] Parthians, and Medes, and Elamites, and the dwellers in Mesopotamia, and in Judaea, and Cappadocia, in Pontus, and Asia, [10] Phrygia, and Pamphylia, in Egypt, and in the parts of Libya about Cyrene, and strangers of Rome, Jews and proselytes, [11] Cretes and Arabians, we do hear them speak in our tongues the wonderful works of God. [12] And they were all amazed, and were in doubt, saying one to another, What meaneth this?

GET
STARTED

Speaking in tongues is not something you do just once to prove you've received the baptism in the Holy Spirit; it's a powerful tool to edify yourself spiritually. Whenever you pray in tongues, you cause yourself to rest, you build yourself up on your most holy faith, and you keep the love of God active and alive in your heart. As you speak forth hidden wisdom and believe for interpretation, revelation knowledge will open up and supply answers you couldn't get any other way. That's why the devil has fought so hard against this gift! He's afraid of what would happen if speaking in tongues ever became part of your daily Christian life.

The Holy Spirit inspires the words, but you have to say them. **"And they were all filled with the Holy Ghost, and began to speak with other tongues, as the Spirit gave them utterance"** (Acts 2:4). Notice that the Spirit gave *them* utterance. It's not just purely the Holy Spirit speaking through you. He gives you a prodding and a desire, but you must do the talking.

It's similar to how the gift of teaching works. If I stood before a group of people and prayed "God, please speak through me, but don't let me say anything that's not of You" and then waited for Him to make me speak, I'd never say anything. It's my responsibility to step out in faith and start talking. God inspires the messages, but they come out through my personality, vocabulary, and mannerisms. God doesn't speak in a Texas drawl; I do! The Holy Spirit supplies the content and I deliver it!

Fear short-circuits your ability to speak in tongues. You might have trouble at first, if you worry about it or try to analyze what you're saying. The Holy Spirit is inspiring you to speak, but it's your fear that's blocking it. Yield your tongue to the Holy Spirit, and then speak forth by faith the words He gives you.

BREAKTHROUGH!

For months, I struggled to pray in tongues. Even though I was convinced it was of God and wanted it, I had a hard time receiving my prayer language.

A man came over to my house in an attempt to help me. He asked, "If you repeated something I said in Spanish, would you be speaking in Spanish?" I nodded. "Then if I spoke something in tongues and you repeated it, would you be speaking in tongues?"

"Yes, but I don't want to just repeat something; I want to speak in tongues on my own!" He kept insisting, so finally I gave in. However, I stopped after only getting through the first couple of words. Embarrassed, I told him I wasn't doing a very good job repeating what he said.

He argued, "Yeah, but you were speaking in tongues. That wasn't English!"

By then I had reached my limit. "No—I don't accept that. I wasn't speaking in tongues!" He just threw up his hands in frustration and left.

Immediately after this, I was on my way to minister to someone. In desperation I declared, "God, I'm just going to start talking. I believe that You are going to help me speak in tongues." Then I began making up nonsense words and saying them out loud. It seemed silly to me, so I didn't feel very good about it. However, I realized that I'd said two words that did sound pretty decent. Since they seemed like a real language to me, I figured they must be tongues. So, I took those two words and started speaking them over and over again all the way to my destination.

Upon arrival, I experienced the best time of ministry I'd ever had before. I was convinced it was because I'd been praying in tongues. On my way home, I started praising God in the car and decided to pray using those two words some more, but I panicked when I couldn't remember them. After struggling so long to pray in tongues, I had forgotten the only two words I'd received!

Then I thought, *I'll just get another two!* So, I started the process over again until another two words came. After using them for a while, I added a couple more. Within a few moments, I was speaking fluently in tongues!

Looking back, I know now that I could have spoken in tongues all along. However, I was under the false impression that the Holy Spirit would come upon me with such force that I wouldn't be able to keep myself from blurting out in tongues. When that never happened, I discovered that He doesn't work that way. The Holy Spirit was just waiting for me to speak out in faith the words He'd been gently inspiring me to say.

Now it's your turn to do the same!

LET'S PRAY

"Father, thank You for baptizing me in the Holy Spirit! I'm so grateful that You gave me this wonderful gift. Please help me to walk in all of its benefits!

"Through speaking in tongues, I can draw on the power You've placed within me: For rest and refreshing, for building my faith and keeping myself in Your love, and for revelation knowledge as interpretation comes.

"I am a believer! Your Word says, 'These signs shall follow them that believe; In my name shall they cast out devils; they shall speak with new tongues (Mark 16:17). By faith, I will speak in tongues from this day forward, in Jesus's name. Amen!"

FATHER IS PROUD OF YOU!

Now, by faith, say out loud those sounds coming up from deep within. You'll be talking in a language unknown to you, but the Holy Spirit is the One inspiring it. You'll be speaking in tongues!

Go ahead—practice awhile! Enjoy yourself in the Lord!

If you aren't fluent right away, don't worry—God is proud of you! When little children start to speak, their parents know what they are trying to say. Even though it's baby talk, they're pleased. Your heavenly Father is proud of you, even if your tongue isn't fluent yet. If you'll just keep using it and not worry about yourself so much, tongues will begin to flow out of you unhindered!

As your brother in the Lord, I welcome you to the Spirit-filled life!

—— OUTLINE ——

I. Speaking in tongues is not something you do just once to prove you've received the baptism in the Holy Spirit; it's a powerful tool to edify yourself spiritually.

    A. Whenever you pray in tongues, you cause yourself to rest, you build yourself up on your most holy faith, and you keep the love of God active and alive in your heart.

    B. As you speak forth hidden wisdom and believe for interpretation, revelation knowledge will open up and supply answers you couldn't get any other way.

    C. The Holy Spirit inspires the words, but you have to say them—**"And they were all filled with the Holy Ghost, and began to speak with other tongues, as the Spirit gave them utterance"** (Acts 2:4).

    D. It's not just purely the Holy Spirit speaking through you—He gives you a prodding and a desire, but you must do the talking.

    E. Fear short-circuits your ability to speak in tongues.

    F. Yield your tongue to the Holy Spirit, and then speak forth by faith the words He gives you.

II. For months, I struggled to pray in tongues—even though I was convinced it was of God and wanted it, I had a hard time receiving my prayer language.

    A. Looking back, I know now that I could have spoken in tongues all along.

    B. However, I was under the false impression that the Holy Spirit would come upon me with such force that I wouldn't be able to keep myself from blurting out in tongues.

    C. When that never happened, I discovered that He doesn't work that way.

    D. The Holy Spirit was just waiting for me to speak out in faith the words He'd been gently inspiring me to say.

    E. Now it's your turn to do the same!

III. By faith, say out loud those sounds coming up from deep within.

    A. You'll be talking in a language unknown to you, but the Holy Spirit is the One inspiring it—you'll be speaking in tongues!

    B. Go ahead—practice awhile! Enjoy yourself in the Lord!

    C. If you aren't fluent right away, don't worry—God is proud of you!

    D. When little children start to speak, their parents know what they are trying to say— even though it's baby talk, they're pleased.

E. Your heavenly Father is proud of you, even if your tongue isn't fluent yet.

F. If you'll just keep using it and not worry about yourself so much, tongues will begin to flow out of you unhindered!

TEACHER'S
GUIDE

1. Speaking in tongues is not something you do just once to prove you've received the baptism in the Holy Spirit; it's a powerful tool to edify yourself spiritually. Whenever you pray in tongues, you cause yourself to rest, you build yourself up on your most holy faith, and you keep the love of God active and alive in your heart. As you speak forth hidden wisdom and believe for interpretation, revelation knowledge will open up and supply answers you couldn't get any other way. The Holy Spirit inspires the words, but you have to say them—**"And they were all filled with the Holy Ghost, and began to speak with other tongues, as the Spirit gave them utterance"** (Acts 2:4). It's not just purely the Holy Spirit speaking through you—He gives you a prodding and a desire, but you must do the talking. Fear short-circuits your ability to speak in tongues. Yield your tongue to the Holy Spirit, and then speak forth by faith the words He gives you.

    1a. True or false: Speaking in tongues is not something you do just once to prove you've received the baptism in the Holy Spirit.
       True
    1b. When you pray in tongues, what three things happen?
       You cause yourself to rest, you build yourself up on your most holy faith, and you keep the love of God active and alive in your heart
    1c. As you speak forth hidden wisdom and believe for interpretation, _____ _____ will open up and supply _____ you couldn't get any other way.
       Revelation knowledge / answers
    1d. Acts 2:4 says, **"And they were all filled with the Holy Ghost, and began to _____ with other tongues, as the Spirit gave them _____."**
       "Speak" / "utterance"
    1e. True or false: Fear short-circuits your ability to speak in tongues.
       True

2. For months, I struggled to pray in tongues—even though I was convinced it was of God and wanted it, I had a hard time receiving my prayer language. Looking back, I know now that I could have spoken in tongues all along. However, I was under the false impression that the Holy Spirit would come upon me with such force that I wouldn't be able to keep myself from blurting out in tongues. When that never happened, I discovered that He doesn't work that way. The Holy Spirit was just waiting for me to speak out in faith the words He'd been gently inspiring me to say. Now it's your turn to do the same!

    2a. Will the Holy Spirit come upon you with such force that you won't be able to keep yourself from blurting out in tongues?
       No
    2b. What is the Holy Spirit waiting for?
       For you to speak out in faith the words He's gently inspiring you to say

3. By faith, say out loud those sounds coming up from deep within. You'll be talking in a language unknown to you, but the Holy Spirit is the One inspiring it—you'll be speaking in tongues! Go ahead—practice awhile! Enjoy yourself in the Lord! If you aren't fluent right away, don't worry—God is proud of you! When little children start to speak, their parents know what they are trying to say—even though it's baby talk, they're pleased. Your heavenly Father is proud of you, even if your tongue isn't fluent yet. If you'll just keep using it and not worry about yourself so much, tongues will begin to flow out of you unhindered!

3a. If you aren't fluent right away, what should you do?
   A. See a speech therapist
   B. Believe to receive the Holy Spirit again
   C. Don't worry
   D. All of the above
   E. None of the above
   C. Don't worry

3b. Is God proud of you, even if your tongue isn't fluent yet?
   Yes

3c. What should you do to get tongues to flow out of you unhindered?
   Keep using it and don't worry about yourself so much

DISCIPLESHIP
——— QUESTIONS ———

1. True or false: Speaking in tongues is not something you do just once to prove you've received the baptism in the Holy Spirit.

2. When you pray in tongues, what three things happen?
   _____
   _____
   _____

3. As you speak forth hidden wisdom and believe for interpretation, _____ _____ will open up and supply _____ you couldn't get any other way.

4. Acts 2:4 says, **"And they were all filled with the Holy Ghost, and began to _____ with other tongues, as the Spirit gave them _____."**

5. True or false: Fear short-circuits your ability to speak in tongues.

6. Will the Holy Spirit come upon you with such force that you won't be able to keep yourself from blurting out in tongues?
   _____
   _____
   _____

7. What is the Holy Spirit waiting for?
   _____
   _____
   _____

8. If you aren't fluent right away, what should you do?
   A. See a speech therapist
   B. Believe to receive the Holy Spirit again
   C. Don't worry
   D. All of the above
   E. None of the above

9. Is God proud of you, even if your tongue isn't fluent yet?

_____

_____

_____

10. What should you do to get tongues to flow out of you unhindered?

_____

_____

_____

ANSWER
—KEY—

1. True

2. You cause yourself to rest, you build yourself up on your most holy faith, and you keep the love of God active and alive in your heart

3. Revelation knowledge / answers

4. **"Speak" / "utterance"**

5. True

6. No

7. For you to speak out in faith the words He's gently inspiring you to say

8. C. Don't worry

9. Yes

10. Keep using it and don't worry about yourself so much

— SCRIPTURES —

ACTS 2:4

And they were all filled with the Holy Ghost, and began to speak with other tongues, as the Spirit gave them utterance.

MARK 16:17

And these signs shall follow them that believe; In my name shall they cast out devils; they shall speak with new tongues.

RECEIVE JESUS AS YOUR SAVIOR

Choosing to receive Jesus Christ as your Lord and Savior is the most important decision you'll ever make!

God's Word promises **"that if thou shalt confess with thy mouth the Lord Jesus, and shalt believe in thine heart that God hath raised him from the dead, thou shalt be saved. For with the heart man believeth unto righteousness; and with the mouth confession is made unto salvation"** (Rom. 10:9-10). **"For whosoever shall call upon the name of the Lord shall be saved"** (Rom. 10:13).

By His grace, God has already done everything to provide salvation. Your part is simply to believe and receive.

Pray out loud, *"Jesus, I confess that You are my Lord and Savior. I believe in my heart that God raised You from the dead. By faith in Your Word, I receive salvation now. Thank You for saving me!"*

The very moment you commit your life to Jesus Christ, the truth of His Word instantly comes to pass in your spirit. Now that you're born again, there's a brand-new you!

Please contact our Helpline (719-635-1111) and let us know that you've prayed to receive Jesus as your Savior. We would like to rejoice with you and help you understand more fully what has taken place in your life. *Welcome to your new life!*

RECEIVE THE HOLY SPIRIT

As His child, your loving heavenly Father wants to give you the supernatural power you need to live this new life.

"For every one that asketh receiveth; and he that seeketh findeth; and to him that knocketh it shall be opened. . . . How much more shall your heavenly Father give the Holy Spirit to them that ask him?" (Luke 11:10 and 13).

All you have to do is ask, believe, and receive!

Pray, *"Father, I recognize my need for Your power to live this new life. Please fill me with Your Holy Spirit. By faith, I receive it right now! Thank You for baptizing me! Holy Spirit, You are welcome in my life!"*

Congratulations! Now you're filled with God's supernatural power!

Some syllables from a language you don't recognize will rise up from your heart to your mouth (1 Cor. 14:14). As you speak them out loud by faith, you're releasing God's power from within and building yourself up in your spirit (1 Cor. 14:4). You can do this whenever and wherever you like!

Please contact our Helpline (719-635-1111) and let us know that you've prayed to be filled with the Holy Spirit. We would like to rejoice with you and help you understand more fully what has taken place in your life.

RECOMMENDED
MATERIALS

TEACHINGS RECOMMENDED IN THIS STUDY GUIDE

LESSON 3 – SPIRIT, SOUL & BODY

Understanding the relationship of your spirit, soul, and body is foundational to your Christian life. You will never truly know how much God loves you or believe what His Word says about you until you do. Learn how the three are related and how that knowledge will release the life of your spirit into your body and soul.

Item Code: 1027-C CD series
Item Code: 1027-D As-Seen-on-TV DVD series
Item Code: 3227-D Live DVD series
Item Code: 318 Paperback
Item Code: 318-A Audiobook
Item Code: 418 Study guide
Item Code: 701 Spanish book
Item Code: 770 Spanish study guide

LESSON 5 – A SURE FOUNDATION

God's Word is the only true foundation for your life. Listen as Andrew explains the supernatural process that occurs when you plant the Word in your heart.

Item Code: 1034-C CD series
Item Code: 1034-D As-Seen-on-TV DVD series

LESSON 7 – ETERNAL LIFE

Is eternal life just about living forever, or could there be more? What does God's Word say? Andrew's answer to this question may change the way you view salvation and your approach to your relationship with God.

Item Code: K60-C Single CD

DISCIPLESHIP EVANGELISM

Did God call us to make converts or disciples? It's an important question. The misunderstanding of that has led to some appalling statistics. Many evangelists now realize that only about 15 percent of those who accept Jesus continue in the faith. It's time we changed our thinking and started practicing what Jesus taught. Learn more in this enlightening series.

Item Code: 1069-C CD series
Item Code: 1069-D As-Seen-on-TV DVD series

THE TRUE NATURE OF GOD

Are you confused about the nature of God? Is He the God of judgment found in the Old Testament or the God of mercy and grace found in the New Testament? Andrew's revelation on this subject will set you free and give you a confidence in your relationship with God like never before. This is truly nearly-too-good-to-be-true news.

Item Code: 1002-C CD series
Item Code: 1002-D As-Seen-on-TV DVD series
Item Code: 308 Paperback
Item Code: 743 Spanish book

YOU'VE ALREADY GOT IT!

Are you trying to get the Lord to heal, bless, deliver, or prosper you? If so, stop it! God has already done all He will ever do for you. How can that be? As Andrew teaches on the balance between grace and faith, you'll understand that you've already got what you need.

Item Code: 1033-C CD series
Item Code: 1033-D As-Seen-on-TV DVD series
Item Code: 320 Paperback
Item Code: 420 Study guide
Item Code: 732 Spanish book

CONTACT INFORMATION

Andrew Wommack Ministries
PO Box 3333
Colorado Springs CO 80934
Helpline: 719-635-1111
www.awmi.net

ABOUT THE ___ AUTHOR ___

Andrew's life was forever changed the moment he encountered the supernatural love of God on March 23,1968. The author of more than thirty books, Andrew has made it his mission for five decades to change the way the world sees God.

Andrew's vision is to go as far and deep with the Gospel as possible. His message goes far through the *Gospel Truth* television and radio program, which is available to nearly half the world's population. The message goes deep through discipleship at Charis Bible College, founded in 1994, which has campuses across the United States and around the globe.